The
Wine Appreciation
Guide

This is a Carlton Book

Text © Robert Joseph 2000
Design and Illustration © Carlton Books Limited

1 3 5 7 9 10 8 6 4 2

This book is sold subject to the condition that it shall not, by way of trade or otherwise, be lent, resold, hired out or otherwise circulated without the publisher's prior written consent in any form of cover or binding other than that in which it is published and without a similar condition, including this condition, being imposed upon the subsequent purchaser.

All rights reserved.

A CIP catalogue for this book is available from the British Library.

ISBN 1 84222 136 1

Project Editor: Vanessa Daubney
Project Art Direction: Brian Flynn
Design: Advantage
Page layout: David Sutton
Picture Research: Lorna Ainger
Production: Lisa French

Printed and bound in Indonesia

THE Wine Appreciation GUIDE

Robert Joseph

Contents

Contents 4

Introduction 6

From Old to New. 8

The Grapes. 12

How Wine is Made. 28

Vintages 44

Reading the Label. 50

Tasting 60

Cooking with Wine. 66

Wine in Restaurants 70

Wine and Health 74

Organic Wine 78

Learning about Wine 82

What to Buy. 86

Facts and Fallacies 94

Picture Credits 96

Introduction

Even before you raise a glass to your lips. Wine has an enormous amount of pleasure to offer. Just look at all those labels on the bottles in your nearest wine shop. A big store may sell anywhere between 5-800 bottles; specialist merchants often offer twice or three times that many, while an internet wine site may list enough to fill the index of an encyclopedia.

All these tempting bottles. Why choose one rather than another? The answer to that question naturally depends on what you plan to do with it. Are you buying wine to drink tonight - or on your new-born child's 21st birthday? Are you looking for a bargain - or for an investment whose value is going to rise over the years? And where are you going to store it? Are you one of the lucky few who live above a cool, damp, dark basement which might have been purpose-designed as a wine cellar? Or are you like most of the rest of us: confronting the challenge of finding the least wine-unfriendly corner of a centrally-heated home that was conceived to suit modern human beings? What about food? Is your wine going to accompany a traditional French casserole, or a "fusion" dish that inventively combines elements from Italy and Asia?

MAKING THE MOST OF YOUR WINE

Food and wine are so wonderfully compatible that it is often easy to overlook one of the most essential differences between them. When you go shopping for meat, fish or vegetables, the chances are that you are looking for ingredients that you are going to combine in some kind of recipe.

Choosing a bottle of wine, however, is more like buying a dish that someone else has already prepared. In simple terms, unless you are going to waste a good bottle of Champagne by mixing it with Guinness to make a Black Lady cocktail, there is very little you can do with a bottle of wine apart from storing, decanting and drinking it. Chopping, stirring, frying and whipping are all a lot more fun to watch than sipping - which, I'd guess, is why far fewer television programmes focus on wine than on cooking.

But if you can't physically do the same kinds of things to wine as you can to food, there are all sorts of ways in which you can change the way that it tastes. Wine evolves over time, sometimes gaining, sometimes losing character and flavour. Pull the cork on a Bordeaux too early and you could end up with a mouthful of tannin. Leave an inexpensive Chardonnay to gather dust in your rack and you'll most likely become the proud owner of a cross between sherry and vinegar that doesn't quite offer the qualities of either.

Different temperatures will affect the way a wine tastes too, in much the same way that a picture frame can affect the look of a painting. An extra few degrees can make a red wine taste soupy, while too long a spell in the freezer could remove all the appeal from your expensive White Burgundy.

Then, of course, there's the business of decanting. If you routinely pour all of your reds into a decanter an hour or so before serving, you'll probably soften lots of tougher young examples pretty effectively, and you'll separate older ones from the sediment that will have settled over the years. But you'll also run the risk of making a frail mature Burgundy or claret so frail that it may not taste of anything at all. Decanting white wine, on the other hand, a practice that is done all too rarely, can for example bring all sorts of flavours out of classy young Chardonnays from Burgundy and the New World.

And finally, of course, we get back to the vexed issue of matching of food and wine. Even the smartest restaurant sommeliers and most sophisticated hosts still often seem to imagine that red Bordeaux will happily accompany a slice of unctuously ripe Brie or Camembert. Anyone who has really focused their attention on this kind of partnership will have discovered that it is downright disastrous for both cheese and wine. Actually, a dry white such as a Sancerre would be a far better choice.

Over the following pages, I'll examine all of these aspects of wine - and a whole lot more - with the simple aim of helping you to get as much pleasure as possible out of every bottle you encounter. So, let's start at the beginning, with a look at how to increase your chances of choosing a wine you are really going to enjoy.

From Old to New

Wine-making is probably the world's second oldest profession. Since long before an unknown Babylonian attached a cylindrical seal to an amphora 6,000 years ago, wine of one kind or another has made people throughout most of the civilized world uproariously drunk, gloriously poetic and thoroughly romantic. More often than not, though, it has quite simply slaked their thirst and made them rather happy.

An essential thing to remember about wine is that, despite the eager efforts of the anti-alcohol campaigners to associate wine with tobacco and almost every other kind of health-endangering drug, it is – or at least it should be – one of the most natural and, when drunk in moderation, healthiest substances man consumes.

Unlike cigarettes, which are a relatively sophisticated human invention, wine more or less created itself. No one knows quite when man – or more probably woman – first discovered this phenomenon, but it could have been at any time since humans became capable of picking and appreciating fruit. According to one legend, it was Noah

Celebrating the god of wine – the "Procession of Bacchus" by Francesco de Mura circa 1760.

who, soon after grounding his ark in what we would now call Turkey, noticed that one of his goats was getting its kicks by nibbling at grapes that had begun to ferment in the sun. Noah became not only the first wine-maker, but also the first wine-drinker; as the Bible says, he "planted a vineyard: and he drank of the wine, and was drunken; and he was uncovered within his tent…". A state with which many a more modern wine-drinker will have ample sympathy.

The Persians agree that the joys of wine were discovered by accident, but disagree on the sex of the discoverer. King Jamshid apparently used to store grapes in jars where they were supposed to turn into raisins that could be eaten during the winter. One jar was set aside as poisonous because its contents were frothy, and it was from this unprepossessing liquid that a young girl, bent on suicide, drew what she thought would be her last drink. Needless to say, a few sips were enough to give her a taste for both life and wine.

From those earliest vintages in what we now call the Middle East, and the first attempts at wine-making in the Caucasian republic of Georgia – where vines are thought to have been cultivated by man in 5,000 BC – the story of wine has unfolded alongside the history of most of the civilized world.

Egypt has never enjoyed a dazzling international reputation for its wines, though archaeologists know they have been made for at least 3,000 years. Nor, despite the current renaissance of the viticulture there, has China. Vines were imported from Persia in 128 BC and some 1,300 years later Marco Polo claimed to have enjoyed drinking the wine they produced. However, many of the other regions we know today, such as Bordeaux, the Rhine and Mosel, had already been established by the time the Romans arrived in Britain in 55 AD.

The Romans took their wines seriously, separating amphorae of different quality and laying down the best vintages for as long as a century. They made sure to have wine to drink wherever they went, even planting vines in England – in Wiltshire, Gloucestershire and London – to save the trouble of importing wine from other parts of the empire. (Unfortunately for those who claim a Roman heritage for English wine, archaeological remains suggest that, then as now, imported wine – principally from Italy, Spain and Germany, and possibly Bordeaux – was far more popular than the stuff made in the vineyards of the chilly new colony.)

A thousand years later, in 1154, King Henry II married Eleanor of Aquitaine and took control of Bordeaux.

The Barossa Valley in Australia offers an ideal climate for Riesling.

Although that region fell out of English hands 300 years later, the relationship was established and "claret" became the "Englishman's drink" it has always remained. Indeed, in the mid-thirteenth century, imports of Bordeaux wine reached the heady figure of over 30 million bottles per year.

As countries and regions quarrelled, made treaties and expelled their religious minorities, over the centuries wine travelled throughout the continent. During this time, most vineyards were in the hands of the church – which explains why English wine-making came to such an abrupt halt in the sixteenth century when Henry VIII dissolved the monasteries, and why, 200 years later, many of France's wine regions were thrown into such turmoil by the anti-clerical decrees of the Revolution.

Politics of another kind helped to create a wholly new style of wine when, following a falling-out between Britain

Barges which once carried the port wine down the Douro river can still be seen moored outside the famous warehouses in Porto.

and France in the seventeenth century, British merchants had to look elsewhere for their red wine. The country they turned to was Portugal, and the wine they found and fortified, to make it more stable for the long sea journey home, was port.

Port was thus essentially a British invention – hence the survival today of British-owned port houses such as Cockburn, Dow's and Taylor's. But this was not the only fortified wine into which the British were dipping their toes. In Jerez, merchants named Williams, Humbert and Harvey created the market for sherry; in Madeira, it was a soldier called Blandy; in Marsala, a Liverpudlian called Woodhouse.

It was also the English who – with the help of the Irish – built up some of the best estates in Bordeaux, as is clear from the names of such illustrious châteaux as Lynch-Bages, Léoville-Barton, Smith-Haut-Lafitte and Cantenac-Brown.

Elsewhere, immigrants from a wide range of countries introduced wine to the New World: the Dutch in South Africa, Spanish missionaries in Chile and California. Sometimes traces of the pioneers' roots are to be found in the wines. In Australia's Barossa Valley, some of the winemakers still speak a dialect of German – and make top-class Riesling. Familiar names such as Heitz, Mondavi and Paul Masson reveal the diverse set of European influences which have helped to create the wine industry in California.

By the late nineteenth century, political disputes

notwithstanding, it appeared as though nothing could stop the progress of wine-making and the trading of wine throughout the western world. Then disaster struck – in the shape of a tiny louse, *phylloxera vastatrix*, whose ideal diet consisted of fresh vine roots.

In its native North America, *phylloxera* caused little damage; there was almost no wine being produced and much of what was made came from a species of vine that was naturally resistant to the louse. The moment it arrived in Europe, however, the louse started behaving like a cake addict in a patisserie. Gradually, but inexorably, it munched its way across the continent.

The Europeans finally admitted defeat and accepted that the only way they could protect their livelihood was by grafting the types of vine they had traditionally grown onto the same kind of resistant stock that flourished naturally in North America. Since the beginning of this century, almost every wine vine in the world – with the exception of those planted in a few areas that are geographically isolated or enjoy some kind of natural protection (the *phylloxera* louse hates sand, for example) – has been grafted onto American rootstock.

The provision of resistant rootstock was the Americans' first contribution to the way wine was made around the world. During this century, since the repeal of Prohibition in 1933, the influence of America – to be more precise, California – has been felt almost everywhere; it is the Californians, more than anyone else, who have developed grape-growing and wine-making from a blend of tradition-bound agriculture and cooking into a highly sophisticated science. And, ironically, in the 1980s it was the Californians who, overestimating the resistance of the rootstocks they had chosen to plant, saw many of their best vineyards devastated by the return of the *phylloxera* louse which had been effectively overcome elsewhere.

Although the number of places where wine is produced has increased enormously, and scientific knowledge and equipment have enabled modern wineries to make more and better wine more consistently than in the past, the fundamental principles are still the same as they were 3,400 years ago, when a man called Kha'y was producing wine for Tutankhamun.

To make good wine, you need the right kind of grapes, the right piece of land, the right climate and the right skills. Today, for example, an Australian wine-maker who talks proudly about his new French oak barrels is, in fact, using pretty much the same kind of casks as the Romans.

And to appreciate wine, all you have to do is to take the trouble to notice how it can differ in flavour and quality – though you might decide not to go as far as the host who, Pliny the Younger wrote, "had apportioned in small flagons three different sorts of wine… . One was for himself and me; the next for his friends of a lower order … and the third for his own freed-men and mine". Nor as far as Richard Nixon who, 2,000 years later, according to Bob Woodward and Carl Bernstein in *All the President's Men*, served visiting congress-men "a rather good six-dollar wine" while he enjoyed "his favourite, a 1966 Château Margaux which sold for about $30 a bottle". Some things never change.

The Grapes

In a world where Chardonnay has almost become just another word for dryish white wine, it is chastening to think that, as recently as the early 1980s, the idea of asking for a wine by the name of the grape rather than the region was still quite novel. Even today wine-drinkers in countries like France, Italy, Portugal and Spain are generally blissfully ignorant of the grapes used to produce their favourite wines. Just stop any middle-aged Frenchman with a supermarket trolley full of bargain bottles of Bordeaux Rouge and Bourgogne Blanc and ask him to name the types of grape from which those wines were made. I'll bet that he will be no more able to provide a correct reply than if you had wanted him to identify one of the more obscure components of the engine of his car.

And that, with few exceptions, is pretty much the way traditional Europeans view grapes – as component parts, of secondary importance to the region in which a wine is made. A Burgundian wine-maker might admit that his Chablis is made solely from Chardonnay grapes, but would never allow it to be sold in a line-up of non-French wines bearing the name of that grape on their label. To him it would be like classing beluga caviar as merely another kind of egg. Besides, he might say, his region's wine is an exception to the rule: most of the classics are blends of different varieties.

In the New World, it is often the other way round. Ask an Australian to point out on a map where the Chardonnay he has just bought was made and he'll most probably admit his ignorance. And you can't really blame him: some of Australia's best-selling Chardonnays simply declare themselves to be the produce of south-eastern Australia, a designation covering all three of Australia's principal wine-making states and some 90 per cent of the nation's vineyards.

The two views appear to be incompatible, but there is a gradual and inexorable coming-together. In France, despite official efforts to ban grape names from the labels of all but a few traditional wines, it is now common to see white Bordeaux describing itself as Sauvignon Blanc. Meanwhile, throughout the New World, there is a growing trend toward creating regional appellations; the wine-makers of Margaret River in Australia and Marlborough in New Zealand, for example, take pains to ensure that their customers are left in no doubt where their respective Sauvignon Blancs are made.

Similarly, while the Chardonnay, Cabernet Sauvignon and Merlot are still the grapes most New-World producers are rushing to plant, they are increasingly being blended with other varieties – often in delicious, but previously unimagined, cocktails.

57 VARIETIES?

There are about 20 different species of grapevine in the world, but only one, *vitis vinifera*, seems to be any good for making wine. There is another, wilder species called *vitis labrusca* which makes usually poor and occasionally unexceptionable wine in the eastern states of North

Harvest-time in Burgundy.

The Grapes

The Riesling grape is a strong contender for the best white grape variety.

America, and a number of hybrids – crosses between *labrusca* and *vinifera* – are grown there and in the UK, but nothing of really fine quality. Other species grow in all sorts of climates, ranging from sub-tropical to Siberian, but *vitis vinifera* flourishes in temperate Mediterranean conditions.

Even within the one species of *vitis vinifera* there are some 5,000 varieties. So, you might suppose, wine could have 5,000 different flavours. But you'd be wrong. Although scientists have isolated thousands of different flavour traces present in wine, there are probably only 50 or 60 grape varieties which can really give a recognizable flavour to the stuff in your glass.

The names of most of these varieties, however, would have been quite unfamiliar to the wine-makers of a century ago, who, accustomed to growing the same grape varieties as their ancestors, viewed imports from other countries and regions with as much suspicion as they might visitors from another galaxy. But just as twentieth-century man mastered the way in which the most successful apples are grown, so he has not only selected the best examples of the most successful types of grape variety for any given set of conditions and propagated them as "clones", but also, by marrying previously separate varieties, developed completely new vines.

A few of these crosses, such as the brilliant grapefruity Scheurebe, are welcome additions to the wine world; others – heavy-cropping and dull-tasting – are about as welcome a creation as the Golden Delicious apple.

Properly used, and in well-judged blends, grapes like the Müller-Thurgau (which was created by crossing the Riesling and Sylvaner) have permitted wine-makers to produce a regular stream of reliable, if sometimes unexciting, wine in regions – such as the British Isles – where neither parent grape naturally flourishes. That's the good news. Unfortunately, this is precisely the same variety with which lazy, greedy producers in northern Germany have often replaced their Riesling – the grape on which their nation's vinous reputation had been built.

The grapes are collected in a vineyard in Nuits St Georges.

RED GRAPE VARIETIES

Baga – The berryish grape of Bairrada in Portugal. Probably that country's best indigenous variety.

Barbera – A grape native to Piedmont, but probably now the most prolifically grown grape throughout Italy, and second in importance there only to the Nebbiolo. However, in the 1980s it suffered a slump in popularity and prestige, and many growers began to replant it with alternative varieties. This was a pity, because the Barbera can make good, fruity, chewy wines, with low tannin and firm acidity, which need far less ageing than many quality Italian reds to show at their best. It's also very versatile, lending itself to a myriad of styles; light or full, dry or sweet, rosé and *frizzante* – even *spumante* – wine. For some observers, the Barbera would have been a far better choice with which to cover the new vineyards of California in the 1990s than the now ubiquitous Merlot. Indeed there are a few American producers, tired of the French grape bandwagon who are growing the Barbera with success. It is also found in former Yugoslavia, Australia – at Brown Bros, for example – and in South America where it flourishes particularly well in Argentina.

Blaufränkisch – Spicy grape exploited with increasing success in Austria, especially in blends with Cabernet.

Bonarda – Grape widely used in Argentina to produce light, quite Beaujolais-like reds.

Cabernet Franc – Generally reckoned to be a lesser grape than its "noble" brother, the Cabernet Sauvignon, the Franc tends to make "greener", "grassier" wine with lighter colour and less obvious tannin. Imagine the smell of blackcurrant leaves, or the taste of barely ripe blackcurrant fruit, and you're well on the way to recognizing Cabernet Franc; or possibly Cabernet Sauvignon grown in a cool climate or often picked prematurely in a country like South Africa. But, given a little warmth, this variety can develop some truly delicious deep, berryish flavours.

It is grown throughout Bordeaux, to be used in blends with the Cabernet Sauvignon, Merlot, small quantities of Petit Verdot and – though rarely nowadays – the Malbec. It is particularly important in the Merlot-dominated vineyards of Pomerol and St Emilion, where some properties (most notably Château Cheval Blanc) make superb Merlot-Cabernet Franc blends from vineyards whose soil is unsuited to the Cabernet Sauvignon.

In the Loire, both Cabernets are grown and often blended to make red and rosé wines labelled simply as "Cabernet". These blends can be delicious, but the big names in Loire reds, Chinon and Bourgueil, are pure Cabernet Franc – as are, the locals say, the best wines of the Touraine region. Here the grape can take on notes of raspberry and strawberry, particularly when it is used in the region's sparkling rosés, most notably Saumur. In Italy, the Cabernet Franc is grown throughout the north, making wines which are dry and light but seem almost sweet in their ripeness. Look out for Grave del Friuli.

New-World examples have been rare, but there are successful efforts at pure, unblended styles in Australia (at the Heritage winery) and California (at Caymus and Carmenet). There is a growing trend toward using it in Bordeaux-style blends – by Australians in Piper's Brook's Tasmanian Ninth Island reds and Lindemans' Pyrus from Coonawarra, and by Californians in a growing range of so-called "Meritage" wines.

Cabernet Sauvignon – The king of red grapes. In the Médoc, in Bordeaux, it is blended with the softer Merlot to produce some of the world's finest, most complex, longest-lived (and most expensive) wines; elsewhere it is similarly successful, used neat or blended with a variety of other grapes.

Rich yet dry, with the smell and flavour of black-currants, cedarwood, green peppers and, occasionally, mint and eucalyptus, its thickish skins help to give it the tannic backbone necessary for long life. Perhaps surprisingly, it is little seen in France outside Bordeaux, except for the Loire, where the cooler climate gives it a grassier tang and, many tasters claim, a characteristic note of green pepper. In Italy it is increasingly used, and increasingly successful, although Italian wine laws have until recently often precluded its wines, and the blends in which it is used, from carrying any designation other than *vino da tavola*. Progressive producers in Portugal, Spain (in Navarra and – experimentally – in Rioja) and even Greece, are using the

Cabernet Sauvignon – used to make some of the finest wine in the world.

grape to great effect too, but the most remarkable European Cabernet Sauvignon success story of recent years in volume terms has been Bulgaria, both in its inexpensive, simple, jammy form and in some rather more serious examples from regions such as Suhindol.

New-World Cabernets range from the ultra-classy to the jammily simple, depending on the prevailing climate and style of wine-making. As a rule, however, Chile produces some of the purest, most blackcurranty examples, Australia makes big, approachable Cabernet (though cooler regions in Victoria and Western Australia are known for lighter, mintier, more berryish versions), California and Washington State a more tannic style (though the 1990s brought a trend toward greater softness), while New Zealand and South Africa's efforts have been light, green and grassy, but better choice of region and harvest date have brought riper flavours.

Cannonau – See Grenache.

Carignan – A black grape widely used for table and dessert wines, mainly in the south of France in regions like Fitou, Corbières and Minervois. If overcropped (as it often is) and fermented carelessly, its wines tend to lack any precise character. When the vines are old and yields low, however, some interestingly toffeeish chocolatey flavours emerge. Carignan also reacts well to the *maceration carbonique* process of fermentation that is used for Beaujolais. It is also grown in South America, North Africa, Israel and southern Spain – more particularly, in the Cariñena area of Aragon,

Spanish harvesters pick up grapes ready to be taken for pressing.

where it is said to have originated. Randall Grahm, ever-enthusiastic fan of otherwise-neglected grape varieties, is justifiably proud of the old-vine Carignan he produces in California.

Carmenere – One of the five varieties that can legally be used to make red Bordeaux, this grape is now almost extinct in that region. Producers found that it ripened unreliably and replaced it with the Merlot, the variety with which it was confused until recently in its new home Chile. With a peppery-toffeeish flavour reminiscent of a blend of Grenache and Merlot, it has great potential for the future. Also known as Grand Vidure.

Cencibel – One of the many Spanish names for the Tempranillo.

Charbono – Rare, spicily intense variety grown in California by brilliant eccentrics like Duxoup.

Cinsault/Cinsaut – Grown in almost exactly the same countries as the Carignan, this is a similarly useful grape, imparting a more spicy, attractive warmth to blends. It is one of the parents of the Pinotage cross grown in New Zealand and South Africa, where the Cinsault is also widely grown, though here it was confusingly traditionally known as the Hermitage. A blend of Cabernet, Syrah and Cinsault is proving successful for Australian and southern French producers, and for Serge Hochar of Château Musar in the Lebanon.

Cot – See Malbec.

Dolcetto – Piedmont's answer to fuller-flavoured Gamay, Beaujolais, this makes full, plum-and-cherryish reds which can be drunk young or after a little wood-ageing. Wines – like Dolcetto d'Alba – are often named after the grape. Best's in Victoria produces a delicious example which makes an interesting comparison with one from, say, Vajra in Piedmont.

Dornfelder – Recently developed grape, used to make some of Germany's most attractive, plummiest reds. Drink young.

Freisa – Unusual floral, mulberryish variety making a comeback in Piedmont, thanks to producers like Bava. Drink this young too.

Gamay – Gamay is Beaujolais. How it is that it can be delicious when grown in a hilly region south of Burgundy, but flat and soupy virtually everywhere else, is a mystery. The colour ranges from darkest pink to medium red, and an unusually blue pigment in the grapes' skins gives young Beaujolais a characteristic violet hue. Its acidity is high, and its taste a mouthful of almost any fresh, ripe red fruit, though cherry is a frequently found flavour. Gamay is best drunk young, though some of the Beaujolais crus age well; with maturity, the Gamay takes on chocolatey-raspberry flavours not dissimilar to the Pinot Noir, to which it is thought to be related. The relationship with the Pinot Noir is given legal recognition in the traditional Bourgogne Passetoutgrain blend and in many wines in Switzerland. Passable Gamay can also be found in the Loire, most successfully as Gamay de Touraine and in Vin de Pays around Lyon. The Napa Gamay and Gamay Beaujolais found in California are different varieties altogether.

Grand Vidure – The Chilean name for the Carmenere.

Grenache – Widely planted in the Rhône, this contributes, on average, a full-flavoured, ripely alcoholic 60 per cent of any Châteauneuf-du-Pape and 100 per cent of the Chateau Rayas, one of that appellation's top wines. With the Syrah, it is the chief component of Côtes du Rhône. Elsewhere in

Grenache – the chief component of Côtes du Rhône.

The Grapes

this region, it is used to make the often disappointing rosés of Provence, Lirac and Tavel, where its essentially peppery tang occasionally shows through, and in the extraordinary red dessert wines of Banyuls in Roussillon.

In Spain, it is known as the Garnacha and, together with the Tempranillo, is one of Rioja's major grapes. It is used to make Cannonau in Sardinia where it may have begun life. California also uses the variety to make mostly forgettable "blush" rosés while "bush" Grenache from the warm Barossa Valley is among the most impressive wines to come out of Australia.

Grignolino – Bright cherryish variety grown in Piedmont and (rarely) in California. Best drunk young.

Kadarka – Earthily tough variety common in Hungary, Bulgaria (where it's called Gamza) and Romania.

Malbec – Spicy variety, now almost expelled from the best vineyards of Bordeaux where it was once part of the standard recipe. Grown in Cahors, (less successfully) as "Cot" in the Loire. For the best examples, though, head for Argentina where it is widely planted and produces deliciously spicy, berryish wines (a little like a cross between Bordeaux and the Rhone), Chile and Australia,

Mataro – See Mourvèdre.

Mavrodaphne – Variety used to make plummy, grapey wine in Greece.

Mavrud – Spicy grape used to some effect in Bulgaria.

Merlot – The success story of the 1990s when it supplanted the Cabernet Sauvignon as America's favourite red wine grape. (Thousands of acres were planted, a wine wittily named Marilyn Merlot was an instant best-seller and Merlot became almost as essential a part of the repertoire as Chardonnay). The Merlot's popularity is explained by its buttery, plummy, toffeed and sometimes slightly minty flavours, its soft texture (there's far less tannin than in Cabernet Sauvignon), and in the prestige it brought from Bordeaux where it is used nearly exclusively to make exotic and ferociously expensive wines such as Château Pétrus and le Pin.

Delicious wines like these, and the few pure Merlots produced in California, are exceptions to the rule, however. Most Bordeaux producers would say that it is best used in

Plump Merlot grapes full of promise.

blends – and best restricted to the clay soil on which it does well (with the Cabernet Franc) in St Emilion and Pomerol. Good producers in these regions use it to produce intense, supple, velvety, plummy, fruit-cake flavours. There are, however, plenty of châteaux making dull earthy wine which does the Merlot no credit at all. Southern French and Italian Merlots are generally unimpressive too, but there are attractively light, juicy wines and a growing number of impressive Bordeaux-like efforts. Elsewhere, any country growing Cabernet Sauvignon will grow Merlot too and good examples have been produced in Spain, Hungary and (by Hatzimichalis) Greece.

Outside California, US producers are making impressive Merlot in Washington and New York states, but good Merlot is rare in Australia. There is a growing number of attractive Merlots in New Zealand, South Africa and Argentina, but the country where it has had the greatest success has been Chile. Unfortunately, the picture is complicated here by the fact that many wines labelled as Merlot are in fact made purely or partly with Carmenere. As attentive readers will have realised, I am far from convinced that vinegrowers have been wise in planting as much Merlot as they have.

The Grapes

The Pinot Noir grape often adds flavour to Champagne.

Morellino – See Sangiovese.

Mourvèdre – Originally from Spain – where it is called Monastrell – this black grape is now most commonly found in the south of France, contributing colour and spice to Châteauneuf-du-Pape, and making solid, fruity, "café" wines in many other Rhône Appellations. In Provence, it provides the fruit in the wines of Cassis, Palette and, notably, Bandol, whose fresh, spicy reds are best drunk young. It has been introduced to the Languedoc to improve more basic *vins de pays* and can now be found in California and Australia under the pseudonym of Mataro.

Nebbiolo – Italy's answer to the Syrah, traditionally making black, dry, tannic Barolo and Barbaresco in the Piedmont hills. More modern-style wines are far fruitier and benefit from the sweetness of new oak barrels. Both can develop gloriously complex flavours with a unique, chocolatey, pruney sweetness – rather like long-forgotten home-made jam – and even a hint of rose petals. More approachable versions are labelled as Spanna, and Nebbiolo d'Alba, for example. While its wines are very different from red Burgundy, the Nebbiolo shares three characteristics with the Pinot Noir. It can be used in a blend, but seems to perform best as a soloist. The flavour and style of its wines are more than usually influenced by the soil and hillside (which is why single-vineyard examples of Barolo and Barbaresco are increasingly common). And, like red Burgundy, wines like Barolo for a long time enjoyed a reputation for being thick and alcoholic which was explained by heavy adulteration with reds made from other varieties far further south.

Elsewhere in Italy, the Nebbiolo swaggers under tough, provocative names like Grumello and Inferno. Brown Brothers makes a good example in Australia and promising efforts are being produced in California.

Periquita – Characterful grape used in Portugal.

Petit Verdot – A spicy, herby variety, used in small (under 10 per cent) doses in Bordeaux where it is thought to ripen unreliably. Michel Rolland has demonstrated at the Marques de Grinon estate that, in a warm climate like La Mancha in Spain, it can make really exciting wines without any help from any other grape. The success of this revolutionary wine has not gone unnoticed by other producers...

Pinot Meunier – Usually restricted to a role in Champagne blends where it is used in most non-vintage wines, but fewer vintage bottlings, this plummy wine is used to make a fascinating light, plummy red at the Best's winery in Australia and at Bonny Doon in California.

Pinot Noir – Probably the world's most sulky and infuriating variety, this home-loving grape has only recently begun to stray successfully beyond its base in Burgundy. Fine (though sadly rare) examples of Burgundian Pinot Noir display extraordinary delicacy and elegance, with characteristic flavours of wild raspberry, strawberry and, occasionally, black cherry when young. With age, they take on chocolatey, gamey, "farmyard" overtones.

If a Champagne has raspberry-chocolatey flavours there's a good chance that it contains a fair proportion of Pinot Noir. In this northerly region of France, most producers don't – thank goodness – even begin to try to turn the grape into a red wine, but blend its clear juice with that of the Chardonnay.

In all but the very warmest years, Alsace and the Loire make thin but passable Pinots but vinify them far more successfully as rosé, particularly in Sancerre. In Oltrepó Pavese the Italians coax it into giving light, smoky, Burgundian-style reds, and Spain is beginning to produce some more creditable efforts. In Germany and Switzerland it also makes light, often almost rosé, wines and in Eastern Europe the Pinot Noir is often used to make sweet reds, though Romania has proved capable of good value dry examples from a clone which might not be pure Pinot Noir.

The New-Worlders have been increasingly successful with the Pinot Noir in Oregon, California (especially in

The Grapes

Carneros, Russian River and Santa Barbara), in the cool regions of Australia (Yarra, Mornington, Tasmania, Pemberton), Chile and South Africa (Hermanus). The "hottest" country for the Pinot Noir, though, might be New Zealand, where it is showing huge promise.

Pinotage – Once quite common in New Zealand, this cross between the Pinot Noir and the Cinsault is now hard to find outside South Africa. Its mixture of spicy Rhone and Burgundian berry flavours can be delicious when the grapes are handled sympathetically by producers like Kanonkop and Grangehurst. The general quality is improving but sadly, there are still far too many "muddy", under-ripe or over-ripe examples to be found.

Ruby Cabernet – A cross between Cabernet Sauvignon and Carignan, used in California and Australia to produce wine like jam made from unripe blackcurrants.

Sangiovese – Chianti, Brunello di Montalcino and Vino Nobile di Montepulciano would be lost without this Tuscan grape, which proliferates throughout Italy yet only achieves greatness in these wines. Its quality and complexity vary enormously, largely because of the number of different clones which exist. At its best, the Sangiovese – or Sangioveto or Morellino, as two of its clones are known – can be the most exciting, herby-spicy grape in Italy – either pure, or in blends with the Cabernet and/or Merlot in so-called "Super-Tuscan" reds. Only the best of its wines can take being aged, though this has not deterred Californians from treating it as a potential flavour of the month in their vineyards. Argentina makes some good examples and Australian producers are experimenting with it.

Spanna – See Nebbiolo.

Syrah/Shiraz – Possibly the most exciting red grape of all, the Syrah – or the Shiraz as it is known in Australia and South Africa – was traditionally vinified singly for great northern Rhône wines such as Hermitage and Côte-Rôtie and used in France to give colour and body to feebler fare from other French regions such as Bordeaux and Burgundy. Legally excluded from this last role by *appellation contrôlée* rules, it still features in Languedoc-Roussillon blends in regions like Minervois. In Australia, it produces decidedly Aussie-style rich, spicy, oaky, intense red such as Penfolds' great Grange and Henschke's Hill of Grace in South Australia as well as the more restrained efforts of wines like Yarra Yering in Victoria, but it also does well in blends with the Cabernet Sauvignon. More recently, a number of wineries in California have successfully introduced the Syrah; examples in South Africa, however, were light and disappointing until recently. Watch out for exciting new wines from here and from Chile, Spain and Italy. Surprisingly, New Zealand seems to be able top get it right occasionally too.

Tannat – Tough, rustic variety used to make Madiran in France and some fair-quality reds in Uruguay.

Tarrango – Recent cross used by Brown Bros and others in Australia to make Beaujolais-style reds.

Teroldego – Juicy grape used to make good-value wines in Italy.

Tempranillo – Found all over Spain under a variety of names (such as Cencibel, Tinto Fino, etc.) and responsible for the strawberryish, soft, relatively light, toffeeish taste of Rioja and much Spanish red. Modern producers like Berberana are proving that, bottled young, the Tempranillo can make lively refreshing wine to compete with Beaujolais, while Miguel Torres marries it successfully to Cabernet Sauvignon. In Argentina, it changes character to produce rather hefty, rustic wine. Plantations of it in France are on the increase and it is beginning to arrive in Australia.

Zinfandel – Thank goodness California has something to

The vines of Sangiovese grapes in Tuscany.

call its own – this is it. A close cousin of the Italian Primitivo, in California, it performs the great vinous feat of being all things to all men. It makes jug wine, fine wine and "port", not to mention its main role these days – sometimes in blends with the Muscat – semi-sweet "white" and "blush" rosé. This last style has become so successful that wine waiters find it hard to persuade some customers that Zinfandel can be red as well as pink. Dry rosé, for which it is ideal, is even trickier to sell. It is also found in small pockets in Australia (Cape Mentelle), South America and South Africa.

Chardonnay – the greatest of the white wine grapes.

WHITE GRAPE VARIETIES

Airén – The world's number-one grape – in terms of hectares planted – grown throughout Spain and, when it is not being distilled into brandy, used to make impressively flavourless wine.

Aligoté – A Burgundy grape which makes freshly acidic white wines that are generally named after the grape and are best drunk young. The most traditional way to drink Aligoté is with cassis (blackcurrant liqueur) in the form of "Kir", a drink which was invented to improve the palatability of the often aggressively acidic wine. It is also grown for still whites in Romania and Russia.

Alvarinho/Albariño - A Vinho Verde bearing the name of this grape is likely to have a fresher, spicier flavour than the rest. In Spain it is known as the Albariño in Galicia and produces small quantities of lovely flowery-spicy wines.

Arneis – Distinctive, spicy-floral variety grown in Piedmont in Italy.

Bacchus – A cross derived from the Riesling, Sylvaner and Müller-Thurgau, displaying many of the characteristics of the last of these, but with a more pronounced, almost Muscatty grapiness. Grown throughout Germany, it is also proving successful in England.

Bouvier – Dull modern grape used in Austria to make late-harvest wines.

Chardonnay – Despite rival claims for the Riesling, this is, by a whisker, the greatest of white wine grapes – and certainly currently the most fashionable. Now grown

White grapes lie ready in the sun for collection.

throughout the world, it has been said by some to have originated in the Lebanon. DNA research has, however confirmed that it is genetically related to its Burgundian neighbour the Pinot Noir. It is in Burgundy that it has traditionally, and indisputably, achieved its finest potential. Even in this region, its flavours can vary enormously from village to village: butter and hazelnut in Meursault, the buttered-digestive-biscuit and ripe fruit of Chassagne-Montrachet, pineappley-fresh in the Mâconnais, flinty and steely in Chablis. When mature, fine Burgundian Chardonnay can also take on a not unpleasant rotty, vegetal richness. The grape also has a natural affinity with oak, which can lend a delicious, toasty complexity to the wine.

Elsewhere in France, the Chardonnay also achieves greatness in Champagne, especially when used "neat" for creamy blanc de blancs. It is grown in the Loire for still and sparkling wines, in the Ardèche and the Jura, and in the rapidly growing vineyards of Languedoc-Roussillon.

In Eastern Europe, the grape has yet to fulfil its promise; in Germany, it can be found in various blends, but is often confused with the Weissburgunder – the Pinot Blanc. The same is true in Italy, where the muddling of the two grapes often obscures the fact that some fine if high-priced Chardonnay is produced. Switzerland and Austria also make passable-to-excellent Chardonnay.

There are good Chardonnays being made in Spain, South America and South Africa, and even India is growing the variety for *méthode champenoise* wines, but it is in California and the Antipodes that most world-class non-Burgundian Chardonnay is to be found. The best of these (such as Kistler, Sonoma Cutrer, Peter Michael) can taste like Burgundy – a trend that is accelerating with the move towards using Burgundian clones and towards allowing the fermentation to be driven by the natural yeasts on the grape skins. Many commercial versions, however tend to be oaky, alcoholic and surprisingly sweet. New Zealand efforts and Australian examples though often reminiscent of tropical fruit and oak are generally drier. The best examples from cooler regions (such as the Adelaide Hills, Yarra and Margaret River) are now of world class. Oregon's Chardonnays are improving too after a disappointing start (thanks to the wrong clone having been planted) and Washington state is making progress, as is Canada.

Chasan – A cross between the Chardonnay and Palomino, used in southern France to make pleasant, commercial sub-Chardonnay wine.

Chasselas – The widely grown Chasselas produces dull white wines – and examples that are subtle and attractively floral. It seems to do best in Switzerland, where it is known as the Dorin or Fendant, and in the Vaud region makes some dry, sturdy whites. In the Loire (where it was supplanted by the Sauvignon Blanc) it is still used for the tiny annual production of Pouilly-sur-Loire. It is also responsible for sparkling Seyssel in the northern Rhône and is found dotted throughout the north and centre of France. It is known as the Gutedel in Germany and grown chiefly in Baden; it is also found in California, under the name Chasselas Doré, and in Algeria and Hungary.

Chenin Blanc – One of the world's trickier grapes, but very widely planted. It ripens late and has a great deal of acidity, with a propensity to bring out the worst in the sulphur dioxide which the wine-makers in its Loire homeland are, in any case, prone to over-use. Good dry examples are rare but can be found in good vintages in Vouvray, occasionally in South Africa (where it is called the Steen), New Zealand and Australia – where it is given the benefit of new oak barrels, which are rarely used in the Loire.

Otherwise, the Chenin's acidity and its vulnerability to *botrytis* – noble rot – provide the essential components for ageing and complexity in the great, sweet wines of the Loire in which the grape reveals honeyed, apple and apricot flavours, and occasionally a smell and taste of wet straw. It also makes an ideal, high-acid base for the Loire's sparkling wines.

Sunset over the Napa Valley in California.

The Grapes

Colombard – Originally from the Charentais in France, where it is still used in Cognac and Armagnac production, the Colombard is now grown in south-west France and Provence to make simple, fresh, fruity wines like Vin de Pays des Côtes de Gascogne which can be good value. It has also been widely adopted for blending in Australia and in California, where it is – to the annoyance of the authorities in France – known as "French Colombard" and – to their further annoyance – used to make "Chablis".

Fendant – Swiss name for – occasionally better than average – Chasselas.

Furmint – Limey grape used to make Tokay in Hungary and, more recently, tangily light dry table wine.

Gewürztraminer/Traminer – One of the most difficult wines to sell, because of its unpronounceability, but one of the easiest grapes of all to recognize "blind", with its perfumed (Parma violets), spicy, exotic fruit (lychee) smells and flavours and oily richness. Supposedly it is a spicy – hence the addition of the German word Gewürz, or "spice" – variant of the Italian Traminer grape. There is now some confusion over the two names, both of which may be applied to the same grape. Some Italian and New-World labels opt for the more easily pronounced Traminer.

The Gewürztraminer is successfully grown in Germany, but is without doubt at its greatest in Alsace, particularly in the *vendange tardive* – late-picked – style. Outside France, in Australia and more particularly in New Zealand, some good "Gewürz" is being made in cooler areas. Look out for good examples from Chile, and for Torres' highly commercial Vina Esmeralda, in whose blend it plays a major role.

Macabeo – Potentially fragrant but more usually dull grape grown in southern France and in Spain where it is also known as the Viura, examples of which are increasingly successful in Rueda.

Malvasia – The grape that produced the vat of Malmsey in which the Duke of Clarence drowned, the Malvasia still makes rich, sweet fortified wine on Madeira, but this originally Greek variety has also for centuries been grown in Rioja, where it not only makes white wine but is also traditionally blended into some reds; the Malvasia is used in this way in France and Italy (where it is an ingredient of DOC Chianti) and now California.

It also makes a wide range of white wines in Italy, Spain and the south of France – dry and sweet, still and frothing – and is used in Portugal for white port. There are plantings, too, in South Africa, South America and California. Good examples can be marmaladey but "stale and nutty" is more often the accurate description.

Marsanne – Chiefly found in the Rhône valley, where it is used with the Roussanne for wines like Hermitage and Côtes du Rhône Blanc. It makes strong, fleshy whites in Cassis in Provence, and dry and sweet, still and sparkling St Péray. Rare but good Australian Marsanne can also be found (at Château Tahbilk and Mitchelton), and it is widely planted (though to little effect) in Algeria. Frustratingly, especially in the Rhône, the Marsanne can make wines which are wonderfully flowery in their youth, and nutty, lemony and rich after a decade or so – but very dull in between.

Melon de Bourgogne – The unexceptional, non-aromatic variety that was onced grown in Burgundy (hence the name) and is now used to make Muscadet – and so-called Pinot Blanc in California.

Moscatel – The Muscat's more workaday brother, with a wide variety of synonyms including Muscat of Alexandria, Gordo Blanco ("the big fat white one") and South Africa's Hanepoot ("honeypot"). It is best used to produce sweet wines, often high in natural alcohol or fortified; some Australian late-harvest Muscats are made from this variety, as is the Portuguese Moscatel de Setúbal, Spain's Málaga, the dessert wines of North Africa and the French vins doux naturels of Lunel and Rivesaltes. The latter rarely compare with those of Beaumes de Venise and Frontignan, made from the "true" Muscat, but can be powerful, if rather heavy-handed, good-value alternatives.

Müller-Thurgau – "Invented" in 1872 by a Dr Müller of Thurgau in Switzerland, who crossed Riesling and Sylvaner vines, this is now shamefully Germany's most widely planted grape and gives soft, flowery gulpability to the great mass of ordinary Liebfraumilch and Niersteiner. It can be capable of more, sometimes managing a passable thumbnail sketch of the Riesling it would like to be, though with a touch of the "cat's pee" smell more usually associated with Sauvignon Blanc.

Perversely, the better examples often come not from the variety's native land but from England and north-east Italy,

The Grapes

where producers treat it with more care, though under its alias of Rivaner there are occasional successes in Germany too.

Muscadelle – An obscure, spicy grape used in white Bordeaux blends and by Australians in its pure state to make Liqueur Tokay in north-east Victoria. Good examples of this smell of fish oil or – more pleasantly – of tea leaves.

Muscat – More accurately called the Muscat Blanc à Petits Grains, this goes under a huge variety of names and is grown all over the world, though the wine it makes tends to share one overriding characteristic – it actually tastes of grapes.

In Alsace, where examples are sadly rare, it is usually dry, but as perfumed and crunchy-fresh as a bunch of the best grapes from the hothouse in autumn. Rosenmuskateller wines from Italy's Alto Adige are less fat, but equally delicious, and some pleasant dry Muscats have been made in the New World, most particularly in Australia which is also the place to find the lusciously powerful, Christmas-puddingy liqueur Muscats of north-east Victoria.

Back in Europe, however, the Muscat is best known in its fortified state as Beaumes de Venise and Frontignan in France or as the golden, liquorous Greek Muscats of Samos and Patras.

The Muscat is also used to make the mouthwateringly grapey French fizz, Clairette de Die. In Italy, as the Moscato, it produces deliciously sweet, much-underrated "playpen" sparkling wines, Asti and Moscato Spumante.

Muscat Ottonel – Just as Eastern and Middle Europe have an inferior alternative to the Riesling, the Welschriesling, so they make wine from this lesser version of the Muscat, the Ottonel. However, in Austria, where it is a particularly important variety, it can make fresh, pleasant wine, and it can also produce very acceptable dessert wines in Romania.

Palomino – A Spanish grape which is enormously important in Jerez, where it is the principal variety for sherry, but grown there and all around the country for dull, dry white table wine.

Parellada – Dull Spanish variety whose use handicaps Cava sparkling wine.

Pedro Ximénez/PX – A very sweet Spanish grape, grown mainly in Andalusia. It makes strong, rich, dark dessert wines – often reaching 16 per cent in alcohol – in Málaga

Pinot Gris, or Grigio, is much grown in Italy and the Alsace.

and, sun-dried and concentrated, produces a sweetening wine for sherry which is sometimes bottled and sold under its own name. In Moriles, Córdoba and other areas of Spain it can be completely fermented to give dry, powerful aperitifs and table wines.

Petit Manseng – Characterful lemony, herby grape used (with the less fine Gros Manseng) for Jurançon and Pacherenc du Vic-Bilh in France.

Pinot Blanc/Pinot Bianco – A grape found in almost every wine-growing region of the world, nearly everywhere producing different flavours and textures, almost none of which inspires real excitement. In France, it is occasionally found in white Burgundies, but is at its rich, slightly nutty best in Alsace and in the Jura, where it makes the unusual *vin de paille*. It is becoming increasingly popular – as the Weissburgunder – in Germany, where it is used both for dry whites and for the more traditional Germanic styles, and over the border almost throughout Italy. In the Alto Adige it makes some sparkling – *spumante* – and good, fragrant, dry wines, though these are often mislabelled as Chardonnay. California, too, claims some examples, though these are probably made from Melon de Bourgogne. It is also grown, though rarely impressively, in Luxembourg, Austria, Chile, Hungary, Uruguay and the former Yugoslavia.

Sauvignon Blanc – one of the most easily recognised white grapes.

Pinot Gris/Pinot Grigio/ Tokay-Pinot Gris – In Italy and Alsace this pink-skinned grape is rapidly becoming a new superstar. As the Pinot Gris it makes pleasant rosés in Touraine, but as Tokay-Pinot Gris in Alsace, it produces lovely, smokily spicy, golden wines, dry or slightly sweet and excellent with food. In Germany it makes good juicy wines in Württemberg, the Pfalz and Baden, and is important, too, for the dry whites from Geneva and the soft dessert wines of the Valais in Switzerland. In Italy, "neat" Pinot Grigios can be deliciously fresh and, blended with Pinot Nero (Pinot Noir), it makes a lovely white from Oltrepò Pavese. It is also found in Abruzzi, and is creeping into the central west area. In Mexico, it makes the "Hidalgo" wines, and it is also grown in the Crimea and for dessert wines in the Murfatlar vineyards of Romania. Occasionally it occurs in Burgundy and it is becoming popular in California, Oregon, Australia and New Zealand.

Riesling – Chardonnay's only rival as the world's top white grape and probably the most wrongly pronounced variety of them all (the first syllable rhymes with Nice the place, not nice the adjective). It is far more versatile than the Chardonnay because it is used to make some of the world's greatest sweet wines as well as some of the steeliest and driest. However, its very versatility makes it far trickier to handle well. In Germany, where it is thought to have originated in the Rhine Valley (hence its often-used pseudonyms, "Rhine" and "Johannisberg" Riesling), it was once almost solely responsible for all of the best dry and sweet wines, but it has recently had to fend off competition from newer varieties such as the Müller-Thurgau.

At their best the Riesling's flavours can combine lime, grape, apple and spice – sometimes baked apple (complete with brown sugar and cloves) can be a very apt description. The variety's great quality is its ability to preserve acidity while building up grapey, honeyed ripeness, enabling fine German wine to age and develop stunningly well. On the other hand, that acidity can be raspingly unwelcome when the grapes are picked unripe, as in some of the Trocken wines from the Rhine. When mature and ripe, really good Riesling can take on a spicy-oily character most usually, and accurately, described as "petrolly" – and delicious.

The Riesling occasionally makes lovely, steely, lemon-fresh wine in Italy's Trentino-Alto Adige region – as it does, more rarely still, in Austria and Switzerland. The "Riesling" grown in Eastern Europe, however, is almost invariably not this noble grape but the inferior Welschriesling (q.v.). Its French home is Alsace, where growers consider it their finest variety. Here, it can make wine with all the freshness, fruit and complexity of German Riesling, but with added weight and dry, fatty fullness.

Australia has by far the most successful dry, off-dry and late-harvest New-World Rieslings – particularly from the Clare Valley and Adelaide Hills – but New Zealand is hot on its heels. In the US, Oregon, Washington state and New York state have all done better with it than California, where it it is sadly being uprooted. South African examples are promising.

Rivaner – Another name for the Müller-Thurgau – and the one by which pioneers in Germany, such as Müller-Cattoir, are labelling some brilliant late-harvest examples of this grape.

Roussanne – More interesting partner to the Marsanne in the Rhône, with a more immediately spicy (though possibly less floral) character.

Sämling 88 – The Austrian name for the Scheurebe grape

The Grapes

Sauvignon Blanc – One of the most easily recognized white varieties – just look for gooseberries, blackcurrant leaf, asparagus or mushy peas in ripe examples and grass and a smell of cat's pee in less ripe ones. France's most famous examples are Loires such as Sancerre and Pouilly-Fumé, but there are also plenty of (often quite ordinary) examples in Bordeaux (where it is blended with the Semillon) and southern France. New Zealand has, since the early 1980s, proved especially adept at bringing out its most pungent flavours – and setting the standard for Chile, South Africa and the cooler regions of Australia. Australians such as Penfolds have innovatively blended the Sauvignon with the Chardonnay – to good effect.

However, despite this instant success, I wonder just how much further the Sauvignon can really go. In the US, for example, though producers in Washington state have released good versions, critics often write it off and many wineries do their best to hide the Sauvignon's true grassy, herbaceous character by using lots of oak (and labelling the wine as *Fumé Blanc*) or by making it very sweet. Unlike the Sémillon, the Sauvignon rarely ages well – unless you like the flavour of tinned asparagus – and is remarkably vulnerable to poor wine-making (in the Loire and Bordeaux in particular). All of which is a great pity, because, at its best, no variety is better suited to partner spicy oriental food, not to mention the new east-meets-west cuisine of California and the Antipodes.

Rülander - The German name for Pinot Gris.

Scheurebe – A Riesling/Sylvaner cross invented in 1916 by George Scheu, this German grape – by far the most interesting modern variety – makes wonderfully and extraordinarily grapefruity white wine. It is used in blends, but is more often made into a varietal wine, particularly in the Auslese style, and in later-harvest versions by the Austrians who call it Sämling 88. The Scheurebe is also one of the most successful grapes to be grown in England.

A bird's eye view of a Hunter Valley vineyard in New South Wales in Australia.

Alsace doesn't just provide picturesque scenes, it also produces some of the best Gewürztraminer.

Sémillon – A split-personality white grape. In Bordeaux, it is used (in blends with the Sauvignon) to make huge quantities of flabby, unrefreshing basic dry white. But it also produces elegant, golden savoury stuff in Pessac-Léognan and wines of exquisite, complex sweetness in Sauternes and Barsac. In Australia, where it is widely planted, it is used in blends with Chardonnay, and produces wonderful, long-lived peachy-lemony wines in the Hunter (where they can be lean and long-lived) and Barossa Valleys, plus luscious late-harvest dessert wine from the Riverina. In cool New Zealand it mimics the Sauvignon, as it tends to in both Chile, South Africa and California (where good examples are, so far, rare). Watch this space.

Sylvaner – An important white grape in terms of planting and production, but an old fashioned and now rather minor variety as regards quality. Its flavour can be rather bland and earthy, and its chief virtue is its ability to provide body and firmness in blends, for which purpose it is widely used in Eastern Europe. Its best wines are made in Alsace (where it is increasingly rare); Germany (particularly in Franken); Italy's Alto Adige, Switzerland and Austria which is thought to be its country of origin.

Torrontes – Muscat-like grape used almost exclusively in Argentina, though also encountered in Spain. Attractive wines which smell sweet and taste dry.

from any of these appellations will owe very little to the basic Trebbiano, and much particular sites and/or clones and to a skilful wine-maker who has fermented it as cool as possible to bring out what little flavour it has – or blended it with more flavoursome varieties. Look also for Tuscany's Galestro, or the superior French dry whites of Bandol and Palette.

Verdejo – A little-known Spanish white grape grown in Rueda where it is contributing to a new wave of fresh, dry wines.

Verdelho – A Portuguese white grape which lends its name to a delicious, dry style of Madeira, the variety is also used in its native country for dry table wine and white port. In Australia, it produces some good, dry, lime-flavoured wines.

Viognier – A rapidly rising star, this white French grape was, until recently, only planted in the Rhône at Château Grillet and Condrieu. Today, however, it is rapidly being introduced to southern France, Australia, Tuscany and, most notably, Australia (Yalumba, Heggies) Chile, Australia and California where it can be delicious (Calera) but is often woefully over-oaked and over-priced. (Some mischievous souls have even suggested that the clone being used may not always be pure Viognier.) At its best, it produces wonderfully perfumed wines with a smell of peaches and apricots, but it is far from easy to produce good and inexpensive examples. Beware of over-production and of wines which have aged poorly.

Viura – More common name for Macabeo – and the one used for successful new-wave whites in Rueda.

Weissburgunder – The German name for Pinot Blanc.

Welschriesling – In Hungary, where it is called the Olasz Rizling, and in north-east Italy, as the Riesling Italico, this grape can produce some sprightly, floral whites; in Austria, it is used not only for light, perfumed dry wines but, when attacked by noble rot, for often impressive versions of Germany's rich, sweet, late-picked styles. But it should never be mistaken for true Rhine Riesling, though its wealth of pseudonyms do their best to encourage confusion. Most Welschriesling rarely rises above accept-able, quaffing "party wine" while Yugoslavia's Laski Rizling is more usually a flabby, sugary disgrace.

Tokay – Australian name for the Muscadelle when it is produced as a fortified wine in north-east Victoria.

Trebbiano/Ugni Blanc – Italy and southern France (where it is called the Ugni Blanc) are heavily planted with this grape, which is one of the most important in Europe in terms of production figures, though not, alas, in quality. It may make superlative Cognac in the Charentais, but, without skilled wine-making and/or unusual clones, it tends to make neutral-tasting, inoffensive white table wine – which is why the vine is the mainstay of basic southern French plonk, pleasantly inoffensive Vin de Pays des Côtes de Gascogne and Italian whites like Orvieto, Soave and Frascati. A good wine

How Wine is Made

God, they say, helps those who help themselves. Well, help yourself to a handful of grapes, crush them, and leave them be for a few days in a reasonably warm place, remove the skins and pips and, hey presto, you'll have made an alcoholic liquid which could legally describe itself as wine. It makes life hard for all those religious anti-alcohol nuts: if God really didn't want us to drink wine, why did He create a self-contained wine-making kit in every grape?

The stuff you've made will probably taste quite foul, of course, but it's only your first attempt, after all, and you've not used much in the way of skill or equipment. All you've done is allow the liquid and the natural sugar within the grape to combine with the millions of yeast cells on the fruit surface which kicked off the natural process of fermentation.

Harvesting grapes for port above the Douro valley.

There are all sorts of ways of managing this process to achieve a particular style of wine, but nothing the wine-maker does can ever influence the ultimate flavour of the stuff in the bottle as much as the raw materials: the type of grapes used, where and how they were grown and harvested, and, of course, the climate.

GRAPE EXPECTATIONS

The grape variety (or varieties – wines are often blends of more than one) used for making any wine is as fundamental to its taste as the type of meat or fish will be to a particular dish. The differences in the flavour of freshly picked Riesling and Gewürztraminer grapes are even more apparent in the wines they are used to make.

Some varieties, such as Burgundy's Pinot Noir and Chardonnay, traditionally perform best as soloists; most, however, are ensemble players, and are more usually found in blends. Claret, for example, is almost always a mixture of two or more varieties, principally the Cabernet Sauvignon, Merlot and Cabernet Franc.

Old World countries' wine laws (Germany being a

Baskets wait to be filled with grapes in the Côte d'Or.

notable exception) prescribe and proscribe certain varieties for each of their designated quality wine areas, based on experience of what grows best there. Only certain grapes – or blends of grapes – may be used to produce a wine labelled with that appellation.

In the New World, rules like these are almost non-existent; producers are free to experiment with as many varieties as they like. The advantage of this approach lies in the way it allows the wine industry to develop new styles without the constraints of potentially irrelevant laws. On the other hand, as consumers have discovered in their high streets throughout the world, a wholly free market rarely favours the demanding, the small and the unfashionable.

Without some kind of appellation system, traditional but little-known grapes like the Gros and Petit Manseng, which are used to make the equally traditional and little-known wine of Jurançon in France, could disappear in the same way as the local butcher and fishmonger.

Good irrigation is often essential for some vineyards.

SOME LIKE IT HOT

Whatever the flavour or fashionability of the grape variety, it will never make decent wine unless it has enough sun to ripen properly. The climatic conditions demanded by wine-making vines are pretty precise.

Ideally, winters should be cold – cold enough for the vine to lie dormant and conserve all its growing energy until the spring when the vine flowers. From this moment until the harvest, the most important element is timely, well measured doses of sun. The all-important final ripening of the grapes should happen in the cooler months of autumn, not all in a rush in the blazing heat of high summer. Too long or hot a blast encourages growth to be too prolific and too rapid to concentrate the subtleties of flavour which can develop naturally through a slower ripening.

The wine-producing regions of the world lie in two quite sharply defined bands: the moderate, temperate zones between 50º and 30º latitude in the northern hemisphere, and 30º and 50º in the southern hemisphere. Within these bands, in general, fine wines are made in the cooler areas furthest removed from the equator. Unless they are carefully handled, grapes from truly warm regions tend to produce large quantities of soft, jammy wine.

However, even within the same latitudes, the climate can vary widely, depending on altitude, distance from the sea and mountains and the influence of such phenomena as the Gulf Stream. To help to define particular local conditions, a Californian scale of "heat units" was devised, based on the average daily temperature during the growing season. This kind of scale tends to underestimate factors such as the difference in day- and night-time temperatures – and just how hot and cold the weather tends to get. Grapes simply do not mature when it is too hot or cool, so high-altitude Idaho, which according to its average temperatures ought to ripen grapes well, cannot usually do so: after a chilly night, they get an hour or so of moderate warmth mid-morning before the noonday heat becomes intense enough to send the fruit off for a self-protective siesta. Elsewhere, on the other hand, in parts of Chile, and the Barossa Valley in Australia, for example, cool nights help to prevent the grapes from becoming over-ripe.

HANDLING THE RAINS

Like any other plant, vines need water to grow properly. If they don't get it, however ideal the rest of the weather, the grapes will be parched and their tough skins will make for hard, tannic red wine. Worse still, a vine which gets no water during crucial periods of its growing season will simply stop growing. On the other hand, what the vines don't need is an untimely storm just before or during the harvest, when the rain will simply dilute the juice of the grapes.

Sometimes these late storms spoil what might have been a fine vintage; sometimes, on the other hand, as throughout the 1990s in Bordeaux, nature meanly subjects the vines to both drought and storms so that the end result is both watery and unripe.

In the New World, Southern France and – more recently – Spain, growers will irrigate the plants to avoid the effects of drought or "stress". French traditionalists in particular, however, dismiss even the most carefully measured irrigation as "industrialized" wine-making and ban it outright. Oddly, they take a more tolerant view when richer château owners hover over their vineyards in helicopters in an elaborate ploy to protect the vines from the ravages of the rain.

The French fear of irrigation per se is unreasonable, as the Bordelais who have gone to make wine in Chile where grapes can-not be grown without additional water would have to admit. But Chile, like Argentina and the more basic vineyards of Australia and California, does offer an object lesson in the dangers of over-irrigation. If your Bordeaux tastes dilute, it's God's fault; if your South American Cabernet Sauvignon is watery, blame the grape-grower.

SITING THE VINEYARD

The way in which the vines are selected, planted and looked after dictates the quality of the fruit they will yield. If the best vineyards are sited in relatively cool areas, to prevent the vine from over-stretching itself, maximum use must be made of the precious – sometimes elusive – summer sun. So the best location for a vineyard in the northern hemisphere is normally on a south-facing slope which, from dawn until dusk, catches as many of the sun's rays as possible.

Vines planted in flat land receive less sunshine, are badly drained, and are prone to frost. The lowest part of the slope is better off, but will suffer from any damp conditions prevailing on the flat land, particularly if there happens to be a stream or river running through it. Vines half-way up the hill receive the most direct sunlight and are well-drained. Higher up, altitude causes cooler temperatures which inhibit ripening. The top of the hill is thus no better than the bottom, suffering from cool temperatures, wind and reduced direct sunlight. In the best wine-growing areas of France, the hilltops are covered by trees.

The vineyards on the slopes either side of the Douro valley can be very steep.

THE LANGUAGE OF THE VINEYARD

Botrytis cinerea – Often called noble rot; in France, *pourriture noble*, and in Germany, *Edelfäule*. Fungus which dehydrates grapes, not only concentrating sugars and acids, but imparting its own characteristic flavour to sweet wines.
Black rot – Fungal disease of both grape and vine due to humid weather conditions.
Bordeaux mixture – Copper sulphate and lime compound used against vine disease.
Canopy management – Modern vine-training methods devised to maximize the quality of the grape.
Chlorosis – Yellowing of the vine leaves through mineral deficiency.
Clone – A selection within a variety of vine taken from one plant exhibiting desirable characteristics.
Coulure – The shedding of flowers or berries, caused by over-vigorous growth, disease or rainstorms at flowering.
Cross – Vine whose parents are two or more varieties within the same species.
Débourrement – The budding of the vines after leaf formation.
Downy – mildew *Peronospera*, a fungal disease. Treated with Bordeaux mixture.
Drip irrigation – New-World method (sometimes computerized) of watering.
Espalier – A method of training vines. Vertical shoots lead off a central trunk of two horizontal stems.
Eutypiose – A fungal infection which withers the vine. Threatens to destroy the world's vineyards as phylloxera did in the late nineteenth century.
Floraison – Flowering of the vine.
Geneva – Double Curtain Method involving training vines along high trellises to maximize sunshine.
Gobelet – Training and pruning of the vine into a bush-like form.
Grafting – The near-universal process of attaching young vines to (phylloxera-resistant) rootstock.
Grey rot or *pourriture gris* – Unwanted botrytis infection.
Guyot (Single or Double) – Common vine-training systems; growth is concentrated into one or two stems.
Hectare – Metric measure equivalent to 10,000 square metres or 2.47 acres.
Herbaceous – The taste of wines made from unripe grapes.
Hybrid – A cross between a vinifera and a labrusca vine.
Leaf-plucking – Process of stripping surplus leaves away to allow more sunlight in to ripen the fruit.
Micro-climate – The precise climate of a vineyard or set of vineyards which will influence the way grapes grow there. Some vineyards, for example, are protected from storms by "rain shadows" created by nearby hills.
Millerandage – Uneven development of grapes within a bunch as a result of cold or wet weather at flowering. Can reduce the size of the crop per vine and thus – sometimes – lead to wine with more concentrated flavours.
Oidium – (Powdery mildew) A fungal disease controlled by sulphur spraying.
Phylloxera vastatrix – Parasitic louse that attacks the roots of the *vitis vinifera* grapevine. It devastated the world's vineyards in the late nineteenth century, since when most vines are grafted onto *phylloxera*-resistant *labrusca* rootstock. Unfortunately, in California, one of the rootstocks used has proved vulnerable to the louse and, in the late 1980s and 1990s, large proportions of the vineyards in the Napa Valley have had to be replanted.
Pruning – The selective trimming of a vine to control its shape and the quantity and quality of its produce.
Rootstock – The rooted part of the vine on to which the scion is grafted.
T-budding – The grafting of one type of vine on to another. A less than ideal means of switching from a commercially unpopular variety to a more saleable one without having to wait the three or four years it takes for new plants to yield their first crop.
Training – The way in which a vine is forced to grow to optimize yield, ripening, ease of harvest etc.
Trie/Triage – Selective harvesting of grapes to pick them at their optimum condition.
Véraison – Final stage in the ripening of the grapes.
Vitis labrusca – US vine species far better for eating and drinking as juice than for wine-making. Never used for quality wine-making.
Vitis riparia – Vine species native to the US and Canada. The wine it produces smells weirdly "foxy". Important for its phylloxera-resistant rootstock and thus used around the world.
Vitis vinifera – The botanical name of the wine-making vine; European varieties are nearly always members of this species.
Yeasts – The "bloom" on grapes is an accumulation of wild yeasts which, left to their own devices, will naturally but unpredictably begin fermentation. New-World wine-makers generally prefer to use cultured yeasts, though some are rediscovering the benefits of allowing natural yeasts to do the job.

You do not have to travel far to realize, though, that this recipe can vary enormously from one quality wine region to another. The vineyards on the banks of the Rhône, Rhine and Douro rivers, for example, often appear steep enough to call for the skills of an amateur mountaineer. The slopes in Beaujolais and Chianti are gentler while those in the Médoc are often hardly noticeable at all, and parts of the valley floors of the Napa and Marlborough Valleys, in California and New Zealand respectively, have a billiard-table flatness.

If a vineyard is particularly prone to frost – as is the case in Chablis, Champagne and the Napa Valley – there are ways to combat it: water sprinklers, oil burners or wind machines to mix in warm air and dispel the cold air lying close to the vines. Over the years, however, man has ingeniously devised non-mechanical methods to improve the environment in which he wants to grow his grapes, draining the soil in Bordeaux and Ontario for example, planting trees as a wind-break in Tasmania and chopping a few of them down in California to allow air to pass through and blow away the pools of cool air which can cause frost. The most dramatic example of this Godlike remodelling of the earth is the E & J Gallo estate in Sonoma where 800 hectares (2,000 acres) were totally re-landscaped before the vines were planted.

THE ANSWER LIES IN THE SOIL

Vine-growing is not unlike gardening: just as you can't grow roses in a garden with unsuitable soil, most varieties of vine have been historically proven to have strong preferences as to where they like growing. These preferences have led French traditionalists to build up a mystique surrounding what they call the *goût de terroir* of their better wines. Translated literally, this refers to the taste of the earth in which the grapes are grown; in fact the term includes other factors such as the physical situation of the vineyard and the climate.

Like most living things (ourselves included), grapes consist largely of water, and so, in turn, does wine. The water content of a grape will inevitably have passed through the soil in which the vine has planted its roots. Different soil types therefore affect the taste of wine as well.

Around the world, the structure of the earth varies considerably. Conditions may repeat themselves, but often a particular region's geology is unique and accounts for the individuality of its wine

The idea, however, that it is the specific minerals in the soil of a given plot of land, which actually contribute to the flavour of a wine made from vines grown there, has come in for increasingly sceptical treatment. Today, the general consensus is that the influence of the soil has far more to do with its natural acidity or alkalinity and its physical structure: the way it holds and reflects heat and its capacity for draining water. Vines, for example, as their growers say, have just as great a dislike of standing around with wet feet as they do of being thirsty.

TENDING THE VINES

Growing vines is farming, just as much as growing barley or rearing pigs, and demands long hours and dedicated attention if the harvest of grapes is to be worth waiting for. Before a vineyard can be planted, it must be prepared and the soil properly turned over and aired. In some instances, it may need to be fumigated; in others growers may decide to correct its acidity or alkalinity.

Next, it is time to plant the vines – a less straightforward business than one might suppose. Unless your chosen site is in a place like Chile, Argentina or parts of the Antipodes which have yet to fall prey to the otherwise ubiquitous *phylloxera* louse, you are almost bound to have to graft your baby plants onto some kind of rootstock that is resistant to the louse.

Rootstock comes in a number of forms, most of which are distinguished by sets of letters or numbers. Until the mid-1980s, the identity of individual types of rootstock was of little interest to growers who merely noted that some were more productive than others. Then came the gradual discovery in the 1980s and early 1990s that AXR, the particular rootstock recommended by the University of California to vine-growers throughout that state, proved – as French experts had predicted in vain – to be less than wholly resistant to the *phylloxera*. Sadly, the damage caused by the louse – over 80 per cent of the Napa Valley vines – was greater than it might have been, because the Californian experts were in denial, initially fooling themselves that the problem didn't exist and then pretending that the louse that was chomping its way

All great vineyards start with the planting of the vines.

A forest of sticks is used for vines trained in the Côte du Rhône.

through the vineyards was a "new biotype" of the *phylloxera*. While their unlucky neighbours replanted their vines on properly resistant rootstock, growers who had wisely disregarded the University's advice by refusing to plant AXR continued to harvest their crops.

Having selected the rootstock, the next task is to choose a clone of the variety you want to grow (see p. 12), the number of vines you are going to plant per hectare and the way you are going to train and prune them.

In the Old World, the density of your vineyard and the method of training will often be pre-ordained by tradition and law. Elsewhere, your decision will depend on the grape variety, the climate – in warm regions you can have fewer vines per hectare – and the style, quality and quantity of wine you want to make.

Methods of training are traditionally adapted to the climates of the countries where the vines are grown. In the late 1980s, though, vine-growers throughout the world began to acknowledge that they might have something to learn from systems of vine "canopy management" developed in New Zealand and Australia by a man called Richard Smart.

In hot countries with limited rainfall, vines are likely to be trained to grow relatively close to the ground, so that the limited moisture available does not have to waste itself on producing too many shoots and leaves, but can be directed into the grapes. In cooler climates, with more rainfall and less sun, priorities are different. Here grapes are usually trained higher, to catch the limited sun more effectively, and reduce the risks of mildew and rot by permitting a free flow of air around the bunches of grapes.

Inevitably, this all paints a very simple picture of what is an extremely complicated subject, with innumerable methods of training and pruning vines. Among those frequently encountered are the Single and Double Guyot, Gobelet, Lenz Moser and the exotically named Geneva Double Curtain, which, needless to say, has nothing to do with Switzerland, but originated in New York State.

Both wooden and stainless steel vats are now used.

FROM VINEYARD TO WINERY

Until quite recently, in the Old World at least, the emphasis has been on the vineyard rather than the winery or cellar. French wine-producers, for example, routinely describe themselves as *viticulteurs* and *vignerons* – both terms which refer to vine-growing – and rarely, if ever, as vinificateurs, the word which most accurately covers the job of converting the grapes into wine.

For many, in both the Old and New Worlds, the task does indeed stop with the harvest; they simply deliver their crop to the local co-operative or bigger winery. But for tens of thousands of smaller estates, picking the grapes only marks the end of a chapter. There's many a slip between the snip of the secateurs and the sip of the wine.

In the 1970s and 1980s, the traditionally conservative world of wine was shaken to its roots by the arrival of technology in the shape of stainless steel tanks to replace the old wooden vats, cooling and heating equipment for the fermentation vats and all manner of high-tech presses and filters – not to mention computers to save human beings from having to watch the gauges and flick the switches.

The wine chemists – the oenologists – and biologists were playing their part too, developing special enzymes and yeast strains to replace the unpredictable stuff found on the skins of the grapes or in the cellars. Taken together, these innovations removed much of the guess-work from the wine-making process, turning, as one Australian gleefully admitted, what was an art or a craft into a science.

If wine-making is a natural process, certain refinements are necessary to make sure that the wine you make tastes good. Present in the white bloom on the skin of grapes are not only good wine yeasts, but tricky wild yeasts and bacteria as well. These are brought to the grapes by insects, or just carried in the air, and are fashionably aerobic – meaning they need plenty of oxygen to work.

If you were to leave fermentation to take place unaided in the open air, the wild yeasts would set to work in a furious rush until they were overcome by alcohol (at a strength of about 4 per cent). The slower-working, but more persistent, wine yeasts would then take over until they had completed the job, leaving the fruits of their labours exposed to the bacteria which feed on alcohol, turning it into vinegar.

Obviously, the bacteria must be prevented from getting a hold, along with the wild yeasts, which work too quickly for the good of the wine. There are two ways of doing this; one is to seal the tanks and starve them of oxygen, and the other is to add sulphur dioxide to the wine juice (or must), which feeds on oxygen and forms an oxygen-exclusive coating on top of the must. These precautions taken, vinification is quite straightforward.

Wine-making is rather like cooking. If the ingredients are fresh and of good quality, and if the basic rules are followed, the final result should be good wine. But just as each cook may have an individual touch, every quality

Machines now help with the collection of the grapes.

How Wine is Made

The use of a conveyor belt, as seen here in Catalonia in Spain, also makes sorting out these white grapes less tedious.

wine-maker will aim to produce wines which bear his own stamp. This he can do by following the rules in his own way.

The temperature of the fermentation, the length of time it is allowed to carry on, the choice of wooden barrels or stainless steel tanks, the age and size of the casks, the period before bottling: all these are factors over which the wine-maker has complete control and which will influence the character of the finished wine.

Much of the fascination of wine-tasting lies in guessing exactly how each particular wine was made. Every glass of wine you drink will have gone through one of the processes described on these pages.

HOW DRY WHITE WINE IS MADE

1. Grapes are picked, possibly by mechanical harvesters which shake them from the vines. They may be sorted; rotten ones are removed. The rest are taken quickly back to the winery. The longer the journey, the greater the risk of oxidation by heat and air.
2. For heavier-bodied wines, grapes may be crushed and allowed to macerate for 24 hours in a cool tank. This "skin-contact" is particularly popular in the New World.
3. For crisp, fruity wines, grapes are lightly crushed and the

How Wine is Made

FLYING WINE-MAKERS

Imagine calling up your favourite Italian restaurant and asking if the chef would mind your sending a young friend into his kitchen to cook dinner for you on your next visit, and every time thereafter. Your friend – an Australian who doesn't even speak Italian – would use the restaurant's ingredients and equipment to prepare precisely the same dishes the chef has been making for years. But he's going to make them the way you want.

Well, hard though it may be to believe, that's the precise equivalent of the proposal Britain's biggest wine-retailers successfully made during the 1990s to dozens of wineries in France (including such classic regions as Bordeaux and Burgundy), Spain, Portugal, Italy, Germany and Eastern Europe, as well, more surprisingly, as such New-World countries as South Africa, Chile and California. Could they send in their own Antipodean "Flying Wine-makers" – young men and women, most of whom arrived shortly before the harvest and left shortly afterward?

What was the secret of these mercenaries of the wine world? And why were they almost all Antipodean? The answer is one of philosophy: unlike many of their Old-World counterparts who tend to let nature and the climate decide on the style of wine produced in any given year, the New-World wine-makers start out with a pretty clear idea of the kind of wine they want to make.

Outsiders also acknowledge that the Flying Wine-makers are readier to work longer hours – no long lunches and weekends off – and to pay greater attention to cleanliness and hygiene than the bosses of the Old-World co-operatives and larger commercial wineries in which they work.

Critics complain that Flying Wine-makers' wines all taste the same; supporters point out that, in blind tastings, and when British and Dutch consumers are allowed to vote with their wallets, it is the interlopers whose bottles regularly win the greatest favour. In 1995, there were over 100 Flying Wine-makers working in Europe; by the end of the century, as winemakers on the ground began to apply the lessons they had learned from the visitors, that figure had dropped by perhaps half, and a growing number of Frenchmen, Italians and Eastern Europeans had reduced the Antipodean emphasis. But, whatever their nationality, the Flying Wine-makers were still playing by what one might call "Australian rules" - producing wines with clean, fruity flavours rather than the grubbiness and earthiness which had once passed for "regional character".

---

solid matter passed straight into the press. Wine-makers may control the temperature, keeping it cool for enhanced crispness.

4. The more you press, the more bitter the result. Some pressed juice is generally added to the "free-run" juice drawn off from the crusher, and the mixture passed into vats. Sulphur is added to kill off bacteria and prevent oxidation.

5. In the vat, suspended matter will drop out of the juice, which can then be allowed to ferment – in vats or in wooden barrels. Modern wineries may use vacuum pumps or centrifuges to separate solids from liquid.

6. In Old-World wineries, the natural yeasts found in the cellars will be responsible for fermentation. New-World and Flying Wine-makers generally prefer to use enzymes and selected cultured yeasts which are more predictable and can, between them, help to give potentially dull wine more flavour though in California in particular there is a welcome trend towards using "natural yeasts" as in Europe.

7. Fermentation may be fast or slow, warm or cool. "Warm" means between 18°C and 25°C; "cool", 18°C. The cooler the fermentation, the fruitier, but possibly less complex, the wine.

8. Barrel fermentation – particularly in small, new oak barrels, as in Burgundy – will give the wine an oaky, vanilla character and some longevity-bearing tannin. This is only appropriate for certain grapes, notably the Chardonnay and Sémillon, and not for more aromatic ones like Muscat and Gewürztraminer. Tank-fermented wine may then go into barrel, or stay in tank.

9. If there is insufficient grape sugar, (powdered) sugar or concentrated grape juice may be added to increase the final alcohol level in a process known as chaptalization. This procedure is banned in most warm regions and supposedly closely controlled in the cool ones. If there's too little acidity

Grape juice flows into a tank ready for the next step in the process.

Workers in Dundee in Oregon in the United States sort through Pinot Gris grapes.

(as is often the case in warm regions), tartaric or citric acid can correct the balance; if there's too much, chalk will remove it.

10. Malolactic fermentation – the natural conversion of (appley) malic acid to (yoghurty) lactic – may take place partially or fully, either of its own accord or with the help of a specially developed innoculum, except where producers want to retain that acidity – as in some New-World styles and Vinho Verde.

11. The wine will then be fined, probably with bentonite, a powdery clay which drags any remaining solid matter, or "lees", to the bottom of the vat or barrel. It will then be "racked" – passed into another vat – before (usually but not invariably) filtering and bottling months or, in some cases, years after the harvest.

12. Some wines, notably Muscadet, are left "sur lie" – on their lees – and so taste slightly yeasty.

13. Inexpensive white wine is often "cold stabilized": chilled so that its tartaric acid forms harmless crystals which can be filtered out rather than be allowed to form in the bottle.

14. If barrels are used, there is the choice of how long the wine remains in them, and what kind and size of barrel to use. Chardonnay gains from being matured in small new oak barrels. Old-fashioned white Dão tends to remain for a long time in large old ones which remove the little fruit flavour with which it was born.

15. Sulphur dioxide is added before bottling to protect the wine. The dose must be carefully judged, otherwise the wine will suffer from a "bad egg" smell.

HOW RED WINE IS MADE

Red wine is made almost exclusively from black grapes, the colour coming from the skins.

1. In some regions – Burgundy for example – grapes are left to macerate in a cool-room or beneath a coating of sulphur for 24 hours or longer before fermentation is allowed/encouraged to begin.

2. All or most of the freshly picked bunches of grapes are first put through a crusher (unless *macération carbonique* is being used – see 4), which just breaks the skins. Depending on the sort of wine to be made, and the amount of tannin required, the stalks may or may not be discarded at this stage.

3. From the crusher, the grapes go straight into the fermentation vats, skins and all. Fermentation can take a few days or up to four weeks or longer to complete, some wine-makers relying on natural yeasts while others prefer cultured ones. The higher the temperature, the more colour and tannin is extracted.

4. To produce youthful, soft, lighter reds, whole grapes are fermented in sealed vats in a process known as carbonic maceration or "whole berry" fermentation. Carbon dioxide trapped in the vat forces the grapes to ferment quickly – sometimes inside their skins – under pressure, and the whole process can be completed in as few as five days. Quite often, modern producers use a "semi-carbonic" system in which some of the grapes are crushed.

5. A wine's colour and tannin content are dictated partly by the length of time the fermenting must remains in contact with the skins and pips. Unless these are restrained under

Despite modern presses some grapes are still crushed by hand.

the surface of the must, by a mesh or other device, they will be carried to the surface of the vat by the carbon dioxide formed during fermentation, and form a "cap" there. If there is no such device, the must is pumped up and over the cap from time to time or dripped through a sprinkler, to break it up and extract colour.

6. To produce bigger, richer reds, the skins may be left in contact with the juice for days or even weeks once fermentation is complete. Paradoxically, this prolonged contact with the tannin-bearing solids can make for softer-tasting wine.

7. If necessary, the must will be chaptalized (see How White Wine is Made).

8. Some Australian wine-makers – unusually – transfer the liquid into barrel before fermentation is complete. This process, which maximizes the effect of new oak on the still-fermenting wine, seems to suit big red styles, though there have been successful, lighter Pinot Noirs made in this way too.

9. The weight of the mass of grapes is sufficient to squeeze the fermented juice out of the grapes, which is then allowed to run into a cask as free-run wine.

HOW WINE IS MADE TO SPARKLE

Sparkling wines are made by every wine-producing country in the world. The carbon dioxide which creates the bubbles in the wine is a natural by-product of fermentation.

If the wine-maker intends his product to be sparkling, he traps the gas in the wine. There it remains dissolved until the pressure is released, when it rapidly makes its way to the surface in the form of tiny bubbles.

There are various ways of capturing fizz in a wine. The best is the *méthode champenoise*, used not only in Champagne but throughout the wine-making world. The way in which the gas is trapped can vary, from a highly skilled, labour-intensive science to a heavy-handed, mass-produced routine, as can the quality of the base wine itself.

The best base wines for sparkling wine are those with high acidity and little character. That the soil (chalk) and climate (cool) of Champagne are ideally suited to producing wines of this type is a major factor in explaining Champagne's pre-eminence among sparkling wines.

The Champagne Method (AKA méthode classique or traditionelle)
Used for: Champagne; Cava; Crémant de Loire, de Bourgogne and d'Alsace; Blanquette de Limoux; quality New-World sparkling wines; Italian "*Metodo Classico*"; quality German Sekt. After the blending of the base wines, a solution of wine and sugar is added, along with specially cultured yeasts, to provoke a secondary fermentation. The bottles are then stacked on their sides in a cool cellar and left for the second fermentation slowly

to run its course. Traditionally, the bottles were then placed, neck first, into specially designed sloping racks, called *pupitres*, where skilled *rémueurs* would, over the course of a few weeks, daily shake, rotate and tilt the bottle slightly to shift the sediment down so that it rested on the cork. Nowadays this job is generally done – many say – just as effectively by machines called *giropalettes*.

Finally the necks of the bottles are chilled, freezing the sediment into a solid plug. When the corks are removed, the plug pops out under the pressure of the carbon dioxide in the bottle. The wine remaining in the bottle is then topped up with more of the same wine and a little liquid sugar, known as the dosage, before being corked with the traditional Champagne cork tied down with wire.

The Transfer Method
Used for: more run-of-the-mill European wines such as Kriter from France; some New-World fizz.

This is essentially a "second-best" cross between the Champagne and cuve close (see below) methods. The second fermentation takes place in the bottle and the wine is transferred under pressure to tanks for *dosage*, filtering and re-bottling.

The Cuve Close, Charmat or Tank Method
Used for: basic French sparklers; all but the best German Sekt; most Asti; Spanish "Granvas" fizz.
Invented by the Frenchman Charmat, this method can make tolerable sparkling wine – ideal, perhaps, for mixing a Buck's Fizz. The base wine is run into huge stainless steel tanks where secondary fermentation takes place at a controlled temperature, followed by dosage, filtering and bottling.

How Wine is Made

METHODS OF FORTIFICATION

The other way to make sweet wines is to add alcohol to the fermenting juice. Those who fortify wine in this way can produce wines – varying in strength from under 16 per cent to as much as 25 per cent – such as port, Marsala, Madeira, the delicious fortified Muscats of Australia and the vins doux naturels of France: Muscat de Beaumes de Venise and Rivesaltes.

With a few exceptions, fortified wines tend to be sweet. This is either because the addition of alcohol was made whilst there was still sugar in the grapes, or because in a few cases – most notably certain sherries – the final result is sweetened.

The French distinguish between *vins de liqueur*, which are made by alcohol being added to the grape juice before it has begun to ferment, and *vins doux naturels*, in which it is added during the fermentation process. Least prestigious of the *vins de liqueur* are the *mistelles*. The best-known are Pineau des Charentes, made in Cognac, Ratafia de Champagne and Floc de Gascogne. Others are used as the base for branded aperitifs.

Of the vins doux naturels, the most popular are the Muscats from the Rhône, Roussillon and Languedoc regions, such as Beaumes de Venise, Rivesaltes and most notably Banyuls, made in Roussillon from the Grenache grape.

Of the other fortified wines, port and Madeira are made by the vin doux naturel method. Sherry is fermented to dryness, then fortified before oxygen and yeasts start to act on the wine.

10. The rest of the bulk goes into a press and is crushed to produce a highly tannic, dark wine. This "press wine" may be added to the free-run wine to add structure to the blend. The wine from both vat and press are transferred to tanks or barrels where the malolactic fermentation (see p. 25) will occur.

11. Red wine generally needs more time to mature than white. The tannin mellows in time, while the other components of the wine have time to blend together harmoniously. Wood barrels are often used for the maturation of red wines and the oak contributes not only additional flavour and complexity but also greater staying power to the wine.

12. In the case of Bordeaux and other blended wines, the "assemblage" will probably take place within a few months of the harvest. It is at this stage that partic-ularly good or disappointing vats or barrels can be set aside for sale separately.

13. "Fine" wine almost always spends at least a year in barrels, large or small, new or old. During this time it must be "racked" (passed from one container to another, leaving the solids behind) to avoid growing stale and almost certainly "fined" with egg-white, which drags suspended yeasts and other solids in the wine downwards. Many quality-conscious producers now choose not to filter their wines to avoid removing flavour, but most commercial reds will pass through a filter before bottling.

14. Finally, time spent in bottle is important, but not every wine needs it. A complex (and expensive) bottle of red will almost certainly benefit from bottle ageing, as will whites with both body and high enough acidity. Simple wines, intended for prompt drinking, will lose colour, freshness and just about everything that makes wine enjoyable, if left for too long.

The delicate blush of rosé wine.

HOW ROSÉ IS MADE

The classic way of making pink wines is to follow the red wine process until about 24 hours into step two. The wine is thus in contact with the black skins for just long enough to become delicately coloured. It is then racked off to complete fermentation on its own. Alternatively, the grapes may be allowed to macerate on the skins for a few hours before they are pressed and vinified like a white wine. The simple addition of red wine to white is illegal for quality still wines in Europe – but permitted for rosé Champagne, and customary for "white" or "blush" Zinfandel which is, in fact, often a blend of red Zinfandel and white Muscat.

Sweet and Fortified Wines

Sweet wines are the most difficult of wines to make and yet can be the best value of any wines in the world. Out of fashion for many years, and still frowned upon by health fascists who would prefer us to consume neither alcohol nor sweetness, good, rich, honeyed white wine is beginning to enjoy a comeback. Quality sweet wine depends on using grape varieties which naturally contain a lot of sugar, picking them late to get all the sweetness of really ripe fruit.

The sugar contained in any grape will, given half a chance and a bit of yeast, ferment into alcohol. The sweeter the grape, the stronger the wine – in theory. In practice, once the strength rises to 15–16 per cent, the alcohol itself will kill off the yeast, leaving you with rather sweet, very alcoholic wine.

So, the key is to stop the fermentation before it gets to this stage. This can be achieved in one of two tricky ways. One method inevitably involves the use of the wine-maker's friend and, occasionally, wine-drinker's enemy – sulphur. Sulphur is needed for almost all white wines, but the sweeter examples need larger doses which, unless they are handled very carefully, give the wines an irritating throat-tickling character. Sadly, while wine-making skills have improved elsewhere, producers of sweet wines are often set in their sulphurous ways. Which is why cheap Sauternes and German late-harvest wines are often so poor – and why

The Varieties of Soil

Each terrain, no matter what it is, can offer pluses and minuses to the wine-maker.

Gravel – A great number of vineyards are perched on the side of river valleys, in well-drained gravel deposits. Vines do better in poor, well-drained soils which make them plunge their roots deeper to find water and goodness. The great wines of Bordeaux come from gravel soils (*Graves* means gravel) which particularly suit the Cabernet Sauvignon. Much depends, however, on the other kinds of soil with which the gravel is combined. If it is over clay, the wine will have less acidity than if it is over limestone.

Granite – The granite vineyards of the southern Rhône, home of Châteauneuf-du-Pape and Tavel rosé, are littered with huge "pudding stones", making the cultivation of anything seem virtually impossible. Once vines are established, however, the stones act as reflectors, bouncing the heat from the sun back on to the grapes. The end result is that they produce big, high-in-alcohol reds and France's most famous dry rosé. In the Beaujolais, granite suits the Gamay; its chemical properties reduce the wine's natural acidity.

Chalk – Chalk, too, makes for very good drainage and forces the vines to work hard for a living. Not all vine varieties like predominantly alkaline soil. Those that do best on chalky hillsides produce white wines of unique character such as the Chardonnay, which forms part of the inimitable blend for Champagne. The keynote of wines made from grapes grown on chalky – limestone – soil is their acidity, a characteristic that links Champagne, Chablis and Sancerre.

Slate – The richer minerals found in slaty soils suit some vines admirably. The alluvial deposits on the banks beside the Rhine and Mosel rivers in Germany are responsible for the delicate fragrance of the gently fruity local wines, produced on the precipitous, barren-looking slopes. The locals say: "Where the plough may go, no great wines grow." The main advantage of slate in regions like the Mosel is its heat retention, which compensates for the low temperatures in which the grapes have to ripen. Slate is also credited with the quality of Rieslings from the far warmer region of Clare in South Australia.

How Wine is Made

THE LANGUAGE OF THE WINERY

Acid – Essential component – in malic (appley) and tartaric form – of wine, giving freshness and bite. Malic acid is naturally converted to the softer (yoghurty) lactic acid via *malolactic fermentation*, which naturally tends to follow the alcoholic fermentation which has turned the sugar into alcohol. Tartaric acid is often added in warm regions.
Alcohol – The by-product of fermentation, created by yeasts working on sugar. It is also added in neutral form during or after fermentation to produce fortified wines. Measured as a percentage of volume.
Anthocyanin – Grape-skin tannin responsible for colour and flavour in red wines.
Autolysis – Interaction between wine and solid yeast matter giving a distinctive flavour, encouraged by ageing wine on its lees in Muscadet and Champagne.
Back-blending – See *süssreserve*.
Barrel-ageing – Maturing of wine in (usually new or newish) oak casks.
Barrel-fermented – Fermented in barrel in order to intensify oak and vanilla flavours.
Barrique – The traditional Bordelais oak barrel, now widely adopted elsewhere, with a capacity of 225 litres (50 gallons). Term used by Italian wine-makers to indicate the use of new oak barrels.
Baumé – See *sugar*.
Bentonite – Clay used for fining.
Blending – The mixing of several wines to create a balanced cuvée. Also called assemblage.
Brix – See *sugar*.
Cap – The floating skins in a red wine must.
Capsule – Once – lead – now foil or plastic – film which covers and protects cork and bottle neck. Wax is also sometimes used – particularly for vintage port.
Carbon dioxide (CO_2) – By-product of fermentation, trapped in wine as bubbles by sparkling wine-makers using the Champagne method, and otherwise induced in or injected into all sparkling wines.
Carbonic maceration – Uncrushed grapes ferment under a blanket of CO_2, intensifying fruit flavours. Also known as "whole-berry fermentation".
Centrifuge – Machine used to separate wine from the lees after fermentation. Also used in production of low-alcohol wines.
Champagne method - See méthode classique.
Chaptalization - See *sugar*.
Chêne - as in "Elevé en Fûts de Chêne" - Refers to barrel-ageing, but not necessarily in new oak.
Concentrated grape must – Grape juice that has been reduced by heating to 20 per cent of its volume. If "rectified", it has also had its acidity neutralized. An alternative to using sugar in *chaptalization*.
Congeners – The colouring and flavouring matter in wines.
Cool fermentation – Temperatures are kept below 18°C (64°F).
Crushing – The gentle breaking of berries before fermentation.
Cryoextraction – A recently developed technique which involves partially freezing grapes before crushing them in order to separate the sweet, flavoursome juice from the water (which freezes more easily). Used in rainy vintages.
Cuvaison – Period of time a red wine spends in contact with its skins.
Cuve – A vat traditionally made of wood used for storage or fermentation.
Cuvée – A specific blend.
Débourbage - Period during which the sediments drop to the bottom of the tank allowing them to be separated from the fresh must.
Egrappoir – Machine which removes stalks from grapes before they are crushed.
Elevage – The "rearing" or maturing of wines before bottling.
Fermentation – The conversion of sugars into alcohol through the action of yeasts.
Filtration – Passing the wine through a medium to remove bacteria and solids (and possibly flavour – which is why some producers prefer not to filter).
Fining – The clarification of must or wine, usually using natural agents such as egg white, gelatine, isinglass or bentonite which, as they sink, attract and drag down impurities (and possibly desirable flavours) with them.
Fortification – The addition of alcohol to certain wines (e.g. sherry and port) either before or after fermentation is complete.
Free-run juice – The clear juice which runs from the crushed grapes before they are pressed. The best-quality juice.
Hectolitre – 100 litres.
Isinglass – Fining agent derived from fish.
Lees – Dead yeasts left after fermentation.
Maceration – Period of contact between wine and skins in red wines.
Maderization – Term for heat-induced oxidation, e.g. in Madeira.
Made wine – Wine made from concentrated must – not fresh grapes.
Malolactic fermentation – Natural or induced conversion of malic acid to the softer lactic acid.
Marc – Skins, stalks and pips left after pressing. May be distilled into brandy.
Méthode champenoise – Now-defunct term replaced by méthode classique.
Méthode classique – The method used in Champagne of inducing secondary fermentation within the bottle in which the wine is sold.
Must – Unfermented grape juice.
Must concentrators – Ingenious machines used to remove water from the juice of grapes picked in the rain. See *cryoextraction*.
Must weight – Amount of sugar in the must.
Mûtage – The addition of alcohol to stop fermentation – used to make sweet fortified wines.
Oak – Preferred type of wood in which to mature wine. Provides character and imparts flavour. Also used in chip form.
Oechsle – See *sugar*.
Oenology – The science of wine-making.
Oxidation – Result of air contact with wine. Controlled in the maturation process; destructive in excess.
Pasteurization – Sterilizing (usually cheap) wine by heating.
pH (number) – Measure of acidity (low) or alkalinity (high).
Press – Machine used gently to squeeze out juice remaining in skins.
Press wine – Blending wine obtained by pressing the grape skins after maceration.
Pumping over – The process of pumping the must over the floating cap of skins to obtain more colour and flavour.
Racking – Decanting from one vessel to another leaving the lees behind.
Skin contact - See *maceration*.
Sugar – The sugar in fresh grape juice is measured prior to fermentation as this will determine the alcohol content and style of wine. Scales of sugar measurement are: in France, Baumé; in the New World, Brix; in Germany, Oechsle. In some regions, sugar may be added to chaptalize the must – to raise its potential alcoholic strength, but not to sweeten it.
Sulphur dioxide (SO_2) – Invaluable antiseptic, antioxidant and preservative. Used sparingly by wise wine-makers.
Süssreserve – In Germany, England and a few other regions, wines can be sweetened by the addition – back-blending – of sweet, unfermented grape juice.
Tannins Extracts – from red grape skins and oak which give a red wine backbone. The mouth-drying quality of cold black tea is due to tannin.
Tartaric acid – See *acid*.
Tartrates - Potassium bitartrate is naturally present in all wine. Most is removed before bottling but some may linger in the form of harmless tartrate crystals.
Varietal - Wine made and named after one or more grape varieties.

The effect of Botrytis, *or "noble rot" as it is sometimes called.*

Austrian, New Zealand, South African, Australian and US wines, though rarely as complex as the best classic examples, are rapidly gaining in popularity.

Wherever a sweet wine is made, ideally it should be produced from grapes affected by "noble rot" – a fungus correctly known as *botrytis cinerea*. Mysteriously, and despite its name, the fungus doesn't actually rot the grapes as much as dehydrate them, breaking through their skins, allowing the water content to evaporate and thus concentrating the richness of the sugar which remains.

In California, where wine-makers have already learnt to master the yeasts which make wine ferment, the aim now is to create great sweet wine every year by spraying rot onto the grapes. Scientists are eagerly devising methods of duplicating exactly the effect of the mould as it creeps over the vines of Bordeaux, the Loire and the Rhine. Purists believe that such pre-empting of nature is cheating, but there are plenty of producers in Sauternes who, in the all-too-frequent years when the *botrytis* fails to form, must feel very tempted to pre-empt nature too.

SEND IN THE CLONES

The idea of propagating human beings from cells taken from a particular individual was first introduced to the general public by the novel and film of Ira Levin's *The Boys from Brazil* – and subsequently by the debate surrounding the "creation" of Dolly the Sheep by scientists in Britain. The ability to create clones of Adolf Hitler may still be the subject of fiction, but vine-growers throughout the world have, since the 1980s, been able to plant identical copies of, say, one of the healthiest, most reliable Chardonnay vines in the Le Montrachet vineyard of Burgundy.

The clone sold by their local nursery will have been reproduced by a process of taking cuttings of successive generations and rejecting any that do not have precisely the same characteristics as the original, until "dissident" examples simply cease to occur. Cuttings taken from the successful strain will always have the desirable features of that original Le Montrachet vine.

Critics of clones complain that planting an entire vineyard with the same clone makes for wines lacking in complexity; most quality-conscious growers recognize this and now opt for a "cocktail" of different clones.

ROLL OUT THE BARREL

Wine-makers have been using oak barrels since the Romans became frustrated with the tendency of amphorae to break. The difference between then and now, however, is that, until the 1970s, the only time they brought in new oak barrels was when the old ones fell apart. This is not to say that no one had realized that in the first three years of their working life, oak casks could add an extra note of sweet vanilla spice to the wines they contained – nor that certain forests produced wood with distinctive and attractive flavours. But the systematic use of oak as an ingredient did not begin until the best châteaux of Bordeaux used the newly acquired funds from the post-war vintages to replace tired casks and New-World wine-makers, eager not to miss a trick, followed in their footsteps...

There is no question that the flavour of oak can improve and add complexity to a wine – and that particular styles of wine work better with particular styles of oak (Rioja and Australian Shiraz do well in American oak while fine Chardonnay prefers wood from the forests of Nevers, Allier or Vosges in France). New barrels are expensive however and, even if "scraped" and re-fired, have a relatively short life. Flying Wine-makers (see p. 25) and others achieve something of the same effect by putting the oak – in the form of chips or "inner stave" planks – in the wine rather than vice versa. For some odd reason, this practice is frowned on by Old-World authorities.

Traditionalists frequently complain about wines being "over-oaked" and even Professor Emile Peynaud, the so-called "father of modern Bordeaux" and the man often credited with and blamed for creating the fashion for new oak, believed that few wines are concentrated and complex enough to support the 100 per cent new oak they are often given.

Thirty years on, Professor Peynaud's suspicion of oak abuse is beginning to strike a chord with wine-makers. In 1995, the innovative Andrew Pirie's Pipers Brook winery in Tasmania won "White Wine of the Year" at the International Wine Challenge with an unoaked Chardonnay, while the first reds made in Chile by Paul Pontallier and Bruno Pratts of Bordeaux were bravely almost devoid of obvious oak flavour. As the 21st century"s first vintages hit the market, the influence of barrels will often be less marked than it was a few years earlier.

Barrels contribute their own "certain something" to the ageing of a wine.

Vintages

One of the greatest areas of wine mystery and mystique is the difference between vintages. Was 1990 a good year for Châteauneuf-du-Pape? When ought I to drink my 1995 claret? Which was better for red Burgundy – 1990 or 1993?

Unfortunately, the closer you look at vintages, the more confusing the subject tends to become; if you want a simple, reliable, easy-to-follow vintage chart that will fit on the back of a credit card, I'm afraid that you are out of luck. If, on the other hand, what you are looking for is good flavour and good value, you've come to the right place – because it's surprising how often the best buys are to be found in years that get the cold shoulder from most vintage charts. The chart on the following pages is different because it looks at drinkability – the readiness of the wine to be enjoyed – as well as quality.

A cellar of which many can only dream.

FRANCE

Bordeaux (Red) Bear in mind the differences between the various regions of Bordeaux – and the differences between what particular wine-makers are trying to produce. A wine simply labelled as Bordeaux Rouge is made for fairly immediate consumption, however good the vintage. At the other end of the scale, a top-class château will normally be aiming to make long-lived wines in good vintages; their "second label" wines (like Château Margaux's "Pavillon Rouge du Château Margaux" and Château Léoville Lascases's "Clos du Marquis") are usually made to be drunk younger than the "first label" wines from the same property and the same vintage.

Type/Region	99	98	97	96	95	94	93	92	91	90	89	88	87	86	85	84	83	82	81	80	79	78	77	76	75	74	73	72	71	70
Northern Haut-Médoc (Pauillac, St-Estèphe, St-Julien)	7△	8△	7△	8△	8△	7△	5●	4●	4●	9△	9▲	8△	4●	8●	8●	3▽	8●	9▲	6▽	5▽	6▽	8●	4▽	6▽	6●	2▽	2▽	2▽	5▽	7●
Southern Haut-Médoc (Margaux)	7△	8△	7△	8△	8△	7△	5●	5●	4▲	8△	8△	8△	5●	8●	8●	4▽	9●	8▲	7▽	5▽	6●	8●	4▽	5▽	7●	2▽	2▽	2▽	5▽	7▽
Graves	7△	8△	7△	8△	8△	7△	6●	5●	4▲	8△	8△	8△	6●	8●	8●	5▽	9▲	9▲	7▽	6▽	7●	8●	4▽	6▽	7●	3▽	3▽	3▽	6▽	8▽
St Emilion/Pomerol	7△	7△	8△	8△	8△	7△	6●	6●	4▲	9△	8△	9△	6●	7●	8●	3▽	8●	9●	7▽	4▽	7▽	7●	4▽	6▽	8▽	3▽	3▽	3▽	6▽	8▽

Bordeaux (White) Until recently, there was very little dry white Bordeaux worth drinking at all – let alone cellaring. Sweet wines from Sauternes and Barsac can, however, last for an extraordinarily long time when they are from top-class châteaux.

Type/Region	99	98	97	96	95	94	93	92	91	90	89	88	87	86	85	84	83	82	81	80	79	78	77	76	75	74	73	72	71	70
Graves	7△	8△	8△	8△	8△	8△	7●	6●	6●	8●	7●	9●	8●	8●	8●	6●	8●	7●	6●	5▽	8●		7▽	4▽	8▽	8▽	4▽	4▽	4▽	8●	8●
Sauternes/Barsac	7△	7△	8△	7△	7△	6▲	3●	3●	5●	8▲	9▲	9▲	5●	8●	7●	3▽	9●	5▽	4▽	5▽	6▽		5▽	2▽	8▽	8▽				8●	7●

Burgundy (Red) Burgundy is possibly the most varied (in quality terms) region in France. As a general rule, the reds of the Côte de Nuits live longer than those of the Côte de Beaune, while the Côte Chalonnaise and the Mâconnais tend to produce wines for younger drinking.

Type/Region	99	98	97	96	95	94	93	92	91	90	89	88	87	86	85	84	83	82	81	80	79	78	77	76	75	74	73	72	71	70	69
Côte de Nuits	7△	8△	7△	8△	8△	5●	6▲	7●	6▲	9●	8●	9●	7●	7▼	9▼	6▽	7▽	7▽	4▽	8▽	7▽	8▽	4▽	7▽		4▽	4▽	8▽	9▽	6▽	8▽
Côte de Beaune	8△	8△	7△	8△	7△	5●	6▲	7●	6▲	9●	8●	9●	7●	7▼	9▼	5▽	7▽	6▽	4▽	7▽	8▽	7▽	3▽	6▽		3▽	3▽	8▽	9▽	6▽	8▽
Côte Chalonnaise/Mâconnais	7△	8△	7△	8△	8△	5●	6▲	7●	6●	9●	8●	8●	7▼	7▽	8▽	5▽	6▽	3▽	7▽	6▽	3▽	6▽				3▽	3▽	8▽	7▽	5▽	8▽

Burgundy (White) Top-class white Burgundy can last supremely well – but don't push your luck by trying to cellar most basic examples for longer than four or five years. In Burgundy, a good vintage for reds can, confusingly, be a poor one for whites – and vice versa.

Type/Region	99	98	97	96	95	94	93	92	91	90	89	88	87	86	85	84	83	82	81	80	79	78	77	76	75	74	73	72	71	70	69
Chablis	8△	7△	8△	8△	9△	7●	6●	7●	5▼	8●	8▲	8▲	7▼	9▼	8▼	7▽	6▽	8▽	7▽	5▽	8▽	8▽	6▽	6▽		5▽	5▽	8▽	9▽	6▽	8▽
Côte d'Or	7△	7△	8△	8△	9△	6▲	6▲	9▲	5▼	9▲	7▲	8▲	7▼	9●	8▼	7▼	6▽	5▽	7▽	5▽	9▽	8▽	6▽	6▽		4▽	6▽	8▽	8▽	6▽	8▽
Côte Chalonnaise/Mâconnais	7△	7△	8△	8△	8△	6●	6●	8●	6▼	8▼	7●	8●	7▽	9▽	7▽	5▽	6▽	7▽	8▽	8▽	5▽										

Alsace Good examples of Alsace can be extraordinarily long-lived – particularly the late-picked Vendange Tardive and Sélection de Grains Nobles wines. However, the region's reds, relatively delicate wines from the Pinot Noir, are for early consumption.

Type/Region	99	98	97	96	95	94	93	92	91	90	89	88	87	86	85	84	83	82	81	80	79	78	77	76	75	74	73	72	71	70	69
Gewürztraminer	7△	7△	9△	7△	7▲	7▲	7●	8●	6●	9●	9●	7●	5▼	8●	9●	3▽	8▼	4▼	6▼	4▼	6▼	4▼	2▼	8▼	7▼	5▼	5▼		8▽	5▽	5▽
Riesling	7△	6△	9△	7△	7▲	6▲	7●	6●	5●	8●	9●	9●		6●	8●	9●	4▼	6▼	5▼	7▼	5▼	7▼	5▼	9▼	8▼	6▼	6▼		9▼	6▼	6▼
Tokay-Pinot Gris	6△	7△	9△	7△	7▲	6▲	7●	7●	6●	8●	9●	9●	5▼	7●	9●	3▼	9▼	4▼	7▼	4▼	6▼	5▼	3▼	8▼	7▼	5▼	5▼		8▼	6▼	6▼

Rhône (Red) Basic Côtes du Rhône, like Beaujolais, is made to be drunk young. Châteauneuf and Gigondas will age better, but for real keeping potential you have to head north to Hermitage, Côte Rôtie and Cornas, some of whose wines are almost undrinkably tough when they are less than five or even 10 years old. These wines, however, are very vintage-dependent, and from lesser years will drink younger.

Type/Region	99	98	97	96	95	94	93	92	91	90	89	88	87	86	85	84	83	82	81	80	79	78	77	76	75	74	73	72	71	70	69
Hermitage	7△	7△	7△	9△	8△	6△	5△	6▲	7△	9△	7▲	8▲	5▽	6●	9▲	6●	9●	8▼	6▼	6▼	6▼	9●	4▽	8▼			6▽	6▽	9▽	8▽	8▽
Côte Rôtie	8△	7△	7△	9△	8△	6△	5△	6▲	7△	8▲	8▲	8▲	7●	6●	9▲	6●	9●	8▼	7●	6▼	6▼	9●	4▽	8▼			5▽	5▽	9▽	7▽	9▽
Cornas	7△	8△	7△	9△	8△	6△	5△	6▲	7△	9△	7▲	8▲	6▽	6●	9▲	5▽	9●	8▼	6▼	6▼	9●	4▽	8●				5▽	5▽	8▽	7▽	9▽
Châteauneuf-du-Pape	7△	8△	7△	8△	8△	6△	6△	5▲	4▼	9△	7●	8●	6▽	6●	8●	5▼	9▼	8▼	7▼	6▼	7▼	9▼	5▽				5▽	5▽	7▽	8▽	8▽

Rhône (White) White Rhônes can be gloriously fragrant when they are young and richly exotic when they are at least a decade old. Between the two stages, although perfectly drinkable, they are for some reason far less attractive than when at either extreme.

Type/Region	99	98	97	96	95	94	93	92	91	90	89	88	87	86	85	84	83	82	81	80	79	78	77	76	75	74	73	72	71	70	69
Hermitage/Condrieu	7△	8△	8△	8△	8●	7●	6●	6●	7▲	8●	9●	8▼	7▽	6▽	8▼	4▽	7▼	8▼	5▽	5▽	6▽	9▼	4▽	6▽							

Champagne Until the 1970s, Champagne vintages were rare; they were only "declared" by producers in what they believed to be exceptional years. Today, thanks to better weather and a keen market, at least a few examples of vintage Champagnes are available almost every year.

Type/Region	99	98	97	96	95	94	93	92	91	90	89	88	87	86	85	84	83	82	81	80	79	78	77	76	75	74	73	72	71	70	69
Champagne		8△	8△	8△		6△	6▲	6▲	10●	9●	8●	5▼	6●	9▼	5▽	7▼	8▼	7▼	5▽	8▽	5▽	4▽	8▽	7▽	4▽	2▽			9▽	8▽	6▽

Vintages

Loire (Red) Although they can have an attractive youthful fruitiness when they are young, good-quality red Loires really do repay keeping.

Type/Region	99	98	97	96	95	94	93	92	91	90	89	88	87	86	85	84	83	82	81	80	79	78	77	76	75	74	73	72	71	70	69
Loire Red	7△	8△	9△	9●	9▲	6●	6●	5▽	4▽	9●	9●	8▽	6▽	8▼	9▼	4▽	7▽	6▽	5▽	6▽	8▽	2▽	9▽	6▽	5▽	3▽	4▽	3▽	6▽	5▽	

Loire (White) Good examples of dry white Loires (Muscadet, Sancerre, Savennières, etc.) can last well, but they rarely improve beyond the first few years. Sweet Loires often need to age to tame their acidity. Many appear to last indefinitely.

Type/Region	99	98	97	96	95	94	93	92	91	90	89	88	87	86	85	84	83	82	81	80	79	78	77	76	75	74	73	72	71	70	69
Coteaux de Layon	6△	8△	9△	9△	9△	8△	4▲	4●	5●	8▲	9▲	8●	4▽	7▽	8●	3▽	7●	5▽	6▽	5▽	6▽	6▽	2▽	9▼	7▽	3▽	4▽	3▽	6▽	3▽	
Vouvray	7△	8△	9△	9△	7△	8▲	4▲	4●	5●	8▲	9●	8●	5▽	9▼	8●	6▽	7●	5▽	6▽	5▽	6▽	6▽	2▽	9▼	7▼	3▽	4▽	3▽	6▽	3▽	

Beaujolais (Crus) Basic Beaujolais and Beaujolais Nouveau should usually be drunk in the year or so after the harvest (nothing awful happens to Nouveau if you don't drink it before Christmas following the harvest). Of the 10 Beaujolais *cru* villages, the ones to keep the longest are Moulin-à-Vent and Morgon, followed by Juliénas and Chénas. Regnié, Chiroubles and Brouilly need drinking up first.

Type/Region	99	98	97	96	95	94	93	92	91	90	89	88	87	86	85	84	83	82	81	80	75	74	73	72	71	70	69	68	67	66
Cru Beaujolais	7△	7△	8▲	7●	7●	7●	7▼	5▽	9▽	7●	8▽	8▽	8▽	5▽	9▽	4▽	7▽	6▽	6▽	5▽										

ITALY

Piedmont Most Barolo needs at least five, if not 10, years to soften enough to be enjoyable. Barbaresco is usually approachable younger.

Type/Region	99	98	97	96	95	94	93	92	91	90	89	88	87	86	85	84	83	82	81	80	79	78	77	76	75	74	73	72	71	70	69
Barolo/Piedmont	7△	8△	8△	8△	9△	8△	7△	5▲	6▲	9△	9△	8●	5▽	7▼	8▲	4▼	6▼	9▲	6●	4▼	8▼	8▼	5▽	5▽	5▽	8▼	6▼		9▼		

Veneto Valpolicella and Bardolino are generally made to be drunk young (though a few exceptions are breaking that rule). *Amarone* and *recioto* keep well, and this applies to white Recioto di Soave as well.

Type/Region	99	98	97	96	95	94	93	92	91	90	89	88	87	86	85	84	83	82	81	80	79	78	77	76	75	74	73	72	71	70	69
Amarone/Recioto Veneto	7△	8△	7△	7△	8△	8△	7△	5△	9▲	9△	6▲	9▲	3▽	8●	9●	5▽	8●	7▽	8●	5●	8▽	8▽	8▽								

Tuscany While Tuscany is usually thought to be the land of Chianti, it is increasingly the place to find exciting wines made from the same varieties as red Bordeaux. These (Sassicaia is a good example) often continue to mature for longer than all but the very best Chianti, most of which is made to be drunk quite young. Many are labelled merely *vino da tavola*, so the name of the wine and producer are important.

Type/Region	99	98	97	96	95	94	93	92	91	90	89	88	87	86	85	84	83	82	81	80	79	78	77	76	75	74	73	72	71	70	69
Chianti/Tuscany	7△	8△	8△	7△	8△	9△	6△	5△	6▲	9●	5●	9●	5●	7●	8●	4▽	7▼	8▼	7▼	4▼	8▼	9▼	7▼	3▽	6▼	4▼	6▽		8▽		

SPAIN

In general Spanish producers indicate their best and better vintages by calling them "*Gran Reserva*" and "*Reserva*" respectively. Both these terms will indicate longer oak-ageing and – in theory – greater potential longevity. Spain produces very few white wines that are built to last.

Type/Region	99	98	97	96	95	94	93	92	91	90	89	88	87	86	85	84	83	82	81	80	79	78	77	76	75	74	73	72	71	70	69
Rioja Reserva/Gran Reserva		8△	8△	8△	8△	9△	5△	7●	8▲	7●	7●	5▽	8●	6●	7●	5▽	7●	9▲	8▼	7▼	6▼										
Penedés (Red)	8△	7△	8△	8△	8△	8△	7△	6●	9▲	7●	7●	7●	9●	6●	8●	5▽	7●	7▽													
Ribera del Duero	7△	8△	8△	9△	8△	9△	5△	6●	8▲	9●	6●	6●	9●	8●	7●	3▽	7●	9●													
Penedés (White)	7△	7△	8△	8●	8●	7●	6●	6●	9●	6●	6●	8●	7▽	6▼	7▼	8▽	7▽	7▽													

PORTUGAL

Like Spain, Portugal makes few long-lived whites. Its reds last better – and are often sold when they are already mature. The term "*garrafeira*" indicates a reserve wine that ought to last well. Vintage port, though always supposedly intended for cellaring, does vary in its likely longevity. Curiously, top-class houses never "declare" a vintage two years running. Most late-bottled vintage port does not develop or improve with age.

Type/Region	99	98	97	96	95	94	93	92	91	90	89	88	87	86	85	84	83	82	81	80	79	78	77	76	75	74	73	72	71	70	69
Bairrada	7△	7△	7△	6△	9△	8△	8△	8△	9▲	5▲	8●	4▼	4▼	7●	4▼	8●	8▼	4▼	8▼	5▼	8▼	5▼	5▼	8▼							
Dão	7△	7△	7△	6△	9△	8△	8△	8△	9▲	6▲	4▼	4▼	7●	4▼	8●	8▼	4▼	8▼	5▼	5▼	5▼	7▼	8▼								
Vintage port		8△			8△	9△		7△	9△				8▲		7▲	6▲		7●				10●			5▽					9▲	

Vintages

GERMANY

The new trend toward "dry", "*Trocken*", wines in Germany complicates the life of anyone trying to draw up a chart like this. These wines – particularly the Rieslings – often take longer to be pleasurably drinkable than their sweeter equivalents, but they don't live as long. Germany's sweetest whites – *Beerenauslesen* and *Trockenbeerenauslesen*, which are mostly made only in the best vintages – can last almost indefinitely.

QbA, Kabinett, Spätlese

Type/Region	99	98	97	96	95	94	93	92	91	90	89	88	87	86	85	84	83	82	81	80	79	78	77	76	75	74	73	72	71	70	69
Mosel	7△	8△	9△	7△	8△	8●	9▲	8▲	7▲	9●	8●	9●	6▽	7●	9▼	6▽	8▼	6▽	6▽	4▽											
Rhine	8△	8△	9△	7△	8△	7△	8▲	8▲	6●	9▲	8●	8●	6▽	7▼	8▼	5▽	8▼	5▽	5▽	6▽											

Auslese, Beerenauslese, Trockenbeerenauslese

Type/Region	99	98	97	96	95	94	93	92	91	90	89	88	87	86	85	84	83	82	81	80	79	78	77	76	75	74	73	72	71	70	69
Mosel	7△	8△	9△	7△	8△	8△	9△	8△	7△	9△	8△	9△	5▲	6▲	9▲		9●														
Rhine	6△	8△	9△	7△	7△	8△	8△	8△	7▲	9△	8▲	8▲	5▲	6▲	9▲		9●														

AUSTRALIA

As in the USA, styles and regions can vary enormously. However, it is fair to say that, while few Australian Chardonnays have been built to last, old Sémillons, Cabernet Sauvignons and Shirazes (and blends of the latter two) can be the longest-lived of all New-World wines.

Type/Region **Red**	99	98	97	96	95	94	93	92	91	90	89	88	87	86	85	84	83	82	81	80	79	78	77	76	75	74	73	72	71	70	69
New South Wales Red	7△	8△	7▲	8▲	9▲	7▲	8●	5●	7●	7●	4▼	8▽	8▽	9▼	8▽	6▽	7▽	9▽	5▽	8▽											
South Australia Red	7△	8△	7▲	8▲	9▲	8▲	8●	6●	8●	8●	5▼	7▼	8▽	8▼	8▽	9▽	6▽	9▽	6▽	8▽											
Victoria Red	8△	7△	8▲	6▲	9▲	8▲	6●	8●	8●	8●	6▼	8▼	8▽	9▼	8▽	7▽	6▽	9▽	6▽	8▽											
Western Australia Red	7△	8△	8▲	8▲	9▲	9▲	7●	7●	7●	8●	6▼	7▼	8▽	8▼	9▽	8▽	8▽	8▽	6▽	8▽											

Type/Region **White**	99	98	97	96	95	94	93	92	91	90	89	88	87	86	85	84	83	82	81	80	79	78	77	76	75	74	73	72	71	70	69
New South Wales White	7△	7△	6●	8●	9●	7●	8●	5▼	8▼	6▽	5▽	8▽	8▽	9▽	8▽	6▽	7▽	9▽	5▽	8▽											
South Australia White	8△	7△	6●	8●	9●	8●	8●	6▼	8▼	8▽	6▽	7▽	8▽	9▽	8▽	8▽	6▽	9▽	6▽	8▽											
Victoria White	7△	7△	8●	7●	9●	8●	6●	8▼	8▼	8▽	6▽	8▽	8▽	9▽	8▽	8▽	6▽	9▽	5▽	8▽											
Western Australia White	7△	7△	8●	8●	9●	9●	7●	5▼	7▼	7▽	6▽	7▽	8▽	8▽	9▽	8▽	8▽	8▽	6▽	8▽											

UNITED STATES

The variation between producers' styles and between grape varieties makes it very difficult to generalize in the USA. And, of course, it is a huge country – California is large and varied enough in itself to warrant an extensive vintage chart of its own. Even so, the following should provide useful guidelines for the more commonly seen wines. The ageability of all but a very few US wines is, as yet, unproven.

Type/Region	99	98	97	96	95	94	93	92	91	90	89	88	87	86	85	84	83	82	81	80	79	78	77	76	75	74	73	72	71	70	69
California Red	7△	8△	7△	7△	8△	7▲	6▲	8▲	9●	9●	7▼	7●	8▼	8▼	9▲	8▼	5▼	7▼	6▽	7▽	6▽	7▽	6▽	7▽	7▽	9▽					
California White	6△	8△	7▲	7▲	8▲	7▲	6▲	8●	9●	8▼	6▼	7▽	7▽	8▽	9▽	7▽	5▽	7▽	8▽												
Pacific North-West Red	7△	8△	7▲	7▲	7▲	7▲	6●	8▲	8▲	8●	8▼	9▽	8▽	7▽	9▽	5▽	9▽	6▽	7▽	9▽	7▽		8▽	7▽	8▽	9▽					
Pacific North-West White	7△	8△	7▲	7▲	8▲	7●	6●	8●	8●	8●	8▼	8▽	8▽	7▽	9▽	5▽	9▽	6▽													

NEW ZEALAND

Reds here are still rarely built to keep successfully, but Chardonnays are already top-class and worth cellaring and Sauvignons last surprisingly well.

Type/Region	99	98	97	96	95	94	93	92	91	90	89	88	87	86	85	84	83	82	81	80	79	78	77	76	75	74	73	72	71	70	69
Red	8△	8▲	8▲	8▲	7●	8●	7●	8●	8●	7●	9●	7●	8▼	7▼	8▼		9▼														
White	8△	7●	8●	8●	6●	8●	6●	8▼	8▼	6▽	9▽	7▽	7▽	8▽	8▽		8▽														

SOUTH AFRICA

Styles here are evolving so fast, and vary so much from producer to producer, that generalization is hard. The best reds seem able to age for a few years.

Type/Region	99	98	97	96	95	94	93	92	91	90	89	88	87	86	85	84	83	82	81	80	79	78	77	76	75	74	73	72	71	70	69
Red	8△	7△	8△	6△	8▲	7●	7●	8●	9●	7●	8▼	7▼	9●	8●	5▼	6●															
White	7△	7▲	8●	7●	7●	7●	7●	7▼	8▼	6▼	4▽	4▽	8▽	6▽	5▽																

When thinking about vintages, it is worth bearing the following points in mind:

- "Great" vintages aren't always the ones you want to buy – particularly if the wines are young and you are going to open them soon. Many "lesser" vintages – such as 1997, 1992 and 1993 for red Bordeaux – are much more enjoyable when they are only a few years old, at an age at which "better" ones – such as 1996, 1995 or 1990 – are not yet ready to drink.

- The quality of a vintage – or lack of it – is only partly dependent on the weather during the summer. The clock begins ticking in the spring when the first leaves appear on the vines, and continues right up until the moment when the last grapes are safely picked and carried into the winery. A spring frost can harm the vines; bad weather at the flowering in the early summer can cut down the size of the crop; rain coupled with warm weather in the summer may lead to rot developing on the fruit; cold temperatures at summer's end may prevent the grapes from ripening properly; storms during the harvest may dilute the wine; hail can tear the bunches from the vines.

- Weather conditions can vary widely within the same country and even region. So, a great year for Burgundy in the east of France may be a rotten one for Bordeaux, down in the south-west. Chablis can have markedly better weather than Chassagne-Montrachet, 100 miles further south – despite the fact that both are usually given the same "White Burgundy" rating on most vintage charts.

- Different grape varieties react in different ways. In Bordeaux, for example, the Merlot – which is the predominant grape in St Emilion and Pomerol – ripens earlier than the Cabernet Sauvignon, which is the main variety in the Médoc. So, in years like 1964, when rainstorms ruined the harvest in the Médoc, the Merlot grapes of the former areas had already been picked in perfectly dry weather. Similarly, the varieties used to make Sauternes and Barsac need damp weather to develop noble rot – the very same damp weather that can cause havoc in neighbouring vineyards where the grapes for dry red wine are grown. Both 1967 and 1965, which were disastrous years for claret, produced

stunning Château d'Yquem. Great years for white Burgundy – 1973, 1979, 1982 and 1986 – are often less impressive for red, partly because the Chardonnay is happier than the Pinot Noir in cooler weather, and partly because, unlike that variety, it has the capacity to produce good wine in heavily productive vintages.

- Wine-makers can get it right in bad years – and wrong in good ones. A week's holiday taken during the crucial week when neighbouring growers discover they have to

Sleeping beauty: one of the finest wines – Château Margaux – lies waiting for a discerning drinker.

spray against rot can make all the difference between making great wine and poor, rotty stuff. Similarly, growers who do not prune tightly enough can allow their vines to over-produce in potentially good vintages and will make thin, dilute wine. If the weather during the harvest is too hot, wine-makers who do not have cooling equipment can see their fermenting vats overheat and their wine irredeemably spoiled.

On the other hand, in rainy years, richer wine-makers can use sophisticated cryoextraction systems to freeze grapes and remove water from the juice and consequently to produce more concentrated wines. Even when not using such new-fangled methods, producers such as the owners of the smarter châteaux in Bordeaux can, in any case, afford to omit all but their best wine from the bottles which will carry the château name. Which helps to explain why, say, in the rainy years of 1997 and 1999, big-name clarets were comparable to those from better, drier vintages while smaller producers made stuff which was downright unacceptable.

Reading the Label

Wine labels are a cross between a passport, with all its legally required information, a visiting card, and a full-scale advertisement for the contents of the bottle. Some are so overloaded with techno-speak that they seem to be aimed at people whose main interest in wine is scientific; others are coy; and some seem to aspire to be thought works of art. But even a label that appears to tell you the bare minimum can be quite revealing: read it carefully and you should know the name of the wine, where and possibly when it was made, the identity of the person or company that produced and/or bottled it, its alcoholic strength and the amount you are getting for your money. And, if you live in an EU country, you will be protected from the kind of labelling featured in our hypothetical example below.

Other labels, more helpfully, may reveal a whole lot more. In the traditional countries of Europe, they might indicate the officially designated quality of the wine (such as *Appellation Contrôlée*, *Premier* or *Grand Cru*) and the style in which it has been made (its sweetness or dryness, and the fact that it is aged in oak barrels, for instance). "New-World" wines from the USA, Australia or elsewhere are more likely to tell you the name of the grape variety from which they are made.

Whatever the wine, and however many helpful or baffling words appear on the label, don't forget that once you know its style, the most important fact about any wine is the name of its producer. Over 1,000 different people make wine labelled as Beaujolais. And they make it to very different standards.

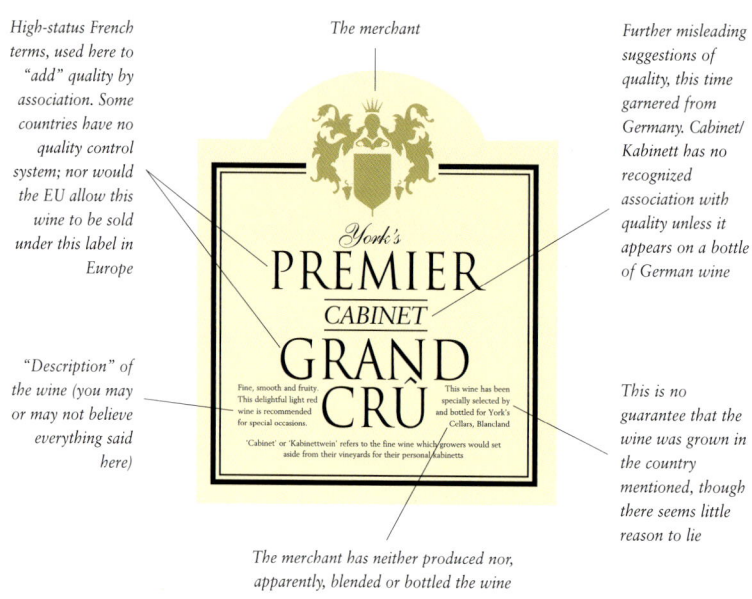

High-status French terms, used here to "add" quality by association. Some countries have no quality control system; nor would the EU allow this wine to be sold under this label in Europe

The merchant

Further misleading suggestions of quality, this time garnered from Germany. Cabinet/Kabinett has no recognized association with quality unless it appears on a bottle of German wine

"Description" of the wine (you may or may not believe everything said here)

This is no guarantee that the wine was grown in the country mentioned, though there seems little reason to lie

The merchant has neither produced nor, apparently, blended or bottled the wine

Reading the Label

- Vintage
- The domaine
- These numbered stamps guarantee the wine's VDQS quality
- Name and address of bottler (obligatory)
- Produce of France, mandatory for all wines that are or may be exported
- The contents by volume. 75 cl is a standard size for EC wines, indicated by the letter "e"
- Alcoholic strength
- Estate-bottled

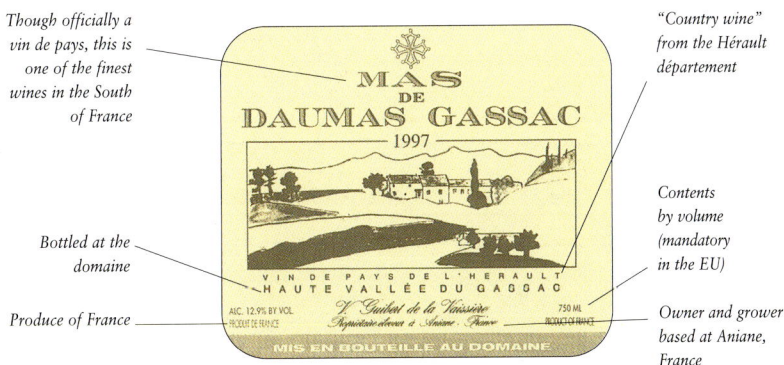

- Though officially a vin de pays, this is one of the finest wines in the South of France
- Bottled at the domaine
- Produce of France
- "Country wine" from the Hérault département
- Contents by volume (mandatory in the EU)
- Owner and grower based at Aniane, France

- A spot of culture: this cuvée takes its name from a Victor Hugo poem, rather than an individual vineyard. Jaboulet has registered both "Le Grand Pompée" and the crest below as trademarks ("marques deposées")
- It is quite common for the "Appellation" to be writ large as the wine's name, then repeated in the standard AC format below
- Contents by volume (mandatory)
- Paul Jaboulet is one of the biggest and best "négociants" in the Rhône; his name is thus printed large as a selling point, as well as appearing with the legally required bottling address below

51

Reading the Label

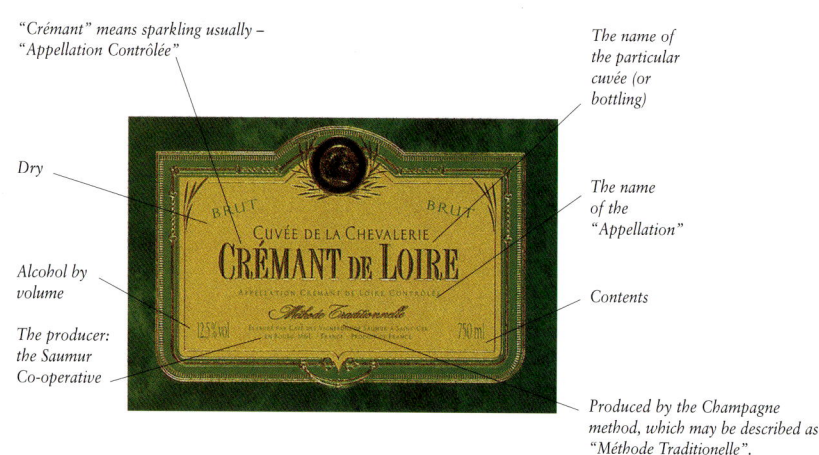

"Crémant" means sparkling usually – "Appellation Contrôlée"

The name of the particular cuvée (or bottling)

Dry

The name of the "Appellation"

Alcohol by volume

Contents

The producer: the Saumur Co-operative

Produced by the Champagne method, which may be described as "Méthode Traditionnelle".

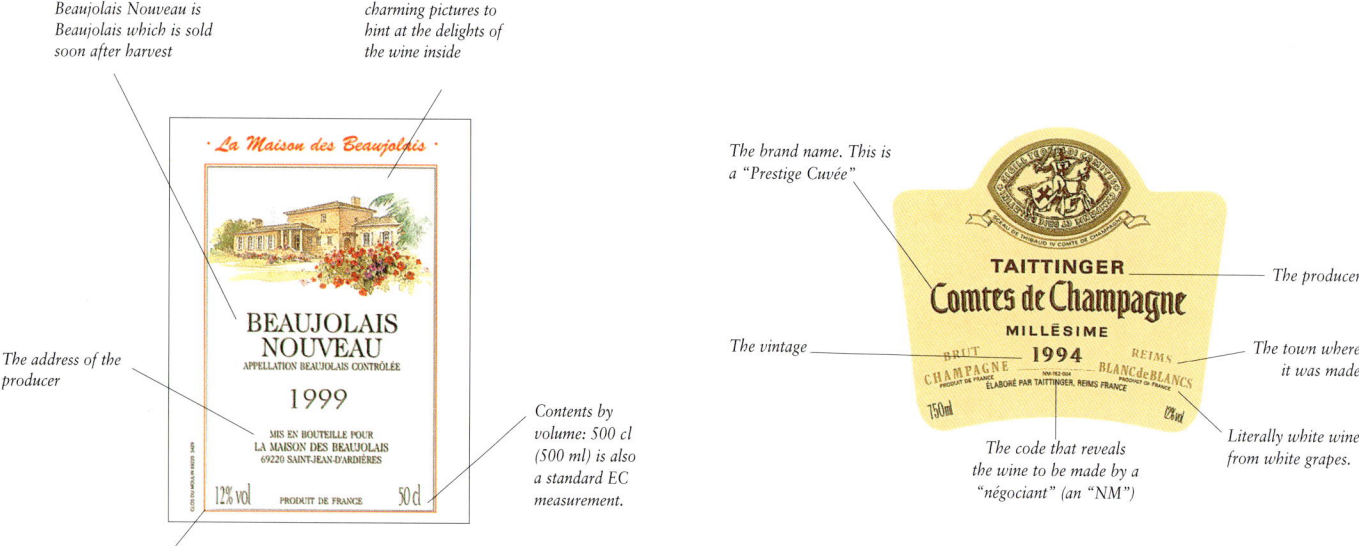

Beaujolais Nouveau is Beaujolais which is sold soon after harvest

Some producers add charming pictures to hint at the delights of the wine inside

The brand name. This is a "Prestige Cuvée"

The producer

The address of the producer

The vintage

The town where it was made

Contents by volume: 500 cl (500 ml) is also a standard EC measurement.

The code that reveals the wine to be made by a "négociant" (an "NM")

Literally white wine from white grapes.

Alcohol by volume

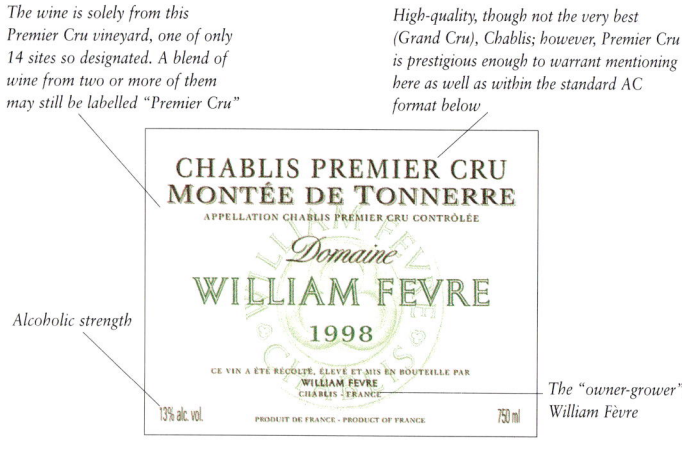

The wine is solely from this Premier Cru vineyard, one of only 14 sites so designated. A blend of wine from two or more of them may still be labelled "Premier Cru"

High-quality, though not the very best (Grand Cru), Chablis; however, Premier Cru is prestigious enough to warrant mentioning here as well as within the standard AC format below

The wine was selected in 1986 by the tasting jury of the Confrérie des Chevaliers de Tastevin, a Burgundian brotherhood that seeks to maintain quality standards

The name of the wine, a basic "Appellation" which can promote some good wines

Wines given the taste vintage label are individually numbered

Alcoholic strength

The "owner-grower", William Fèvre

Contents

"Appellation Contrôlée"

Rodet is a "négociant" – merchant – based at Mercurey

Producer

52

Reading the Label

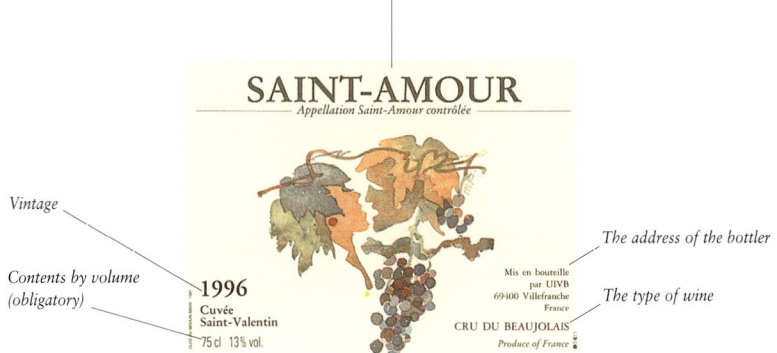

The Appellation is used here as the name of the wine as well as to show its origin below.

Vintage

Contents by volume (obligatory)

The address of the bottler

The type of wine

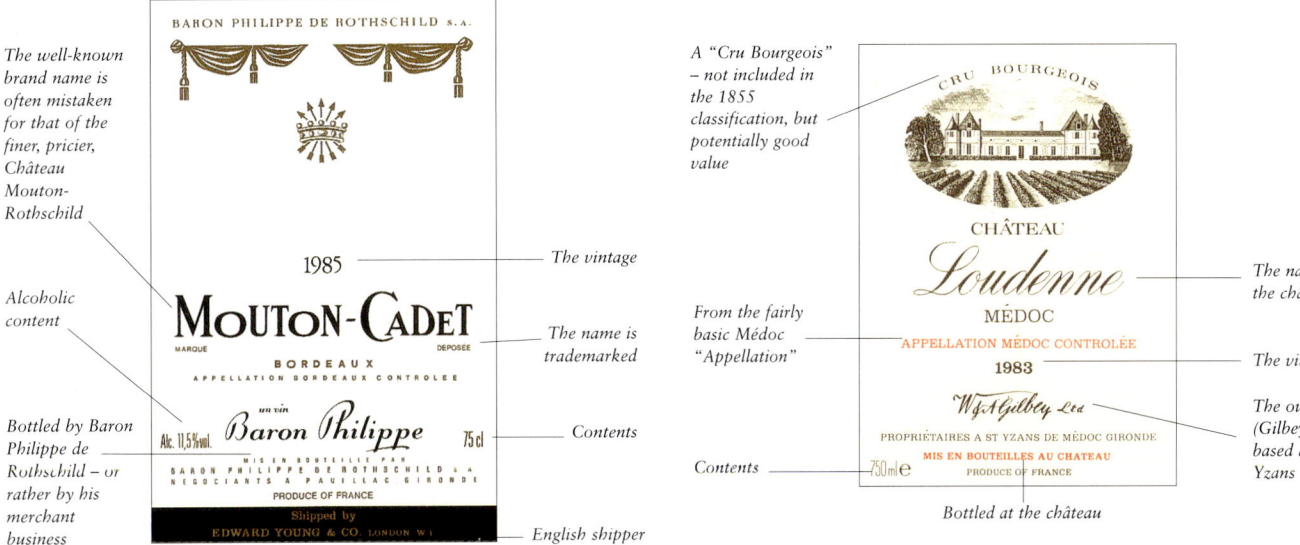

The well-known brand name is often mistaken for that of the finer, pricier, Château Mouton-Rothschild

Alcoholic content

Bottled by Baron Philippe de Rothschild – or rather by his merchant business

The vintage

The name is trademarked

Contents

English shipper

A "Cru Bourgeois" – not included in the 1855 classification, but potentially good value

From the fairly basic Médoc "Appellation"

Contents

The name of the château

The vintage

The owners (Gilbeys) are based at St Yzans

Bottled at the château

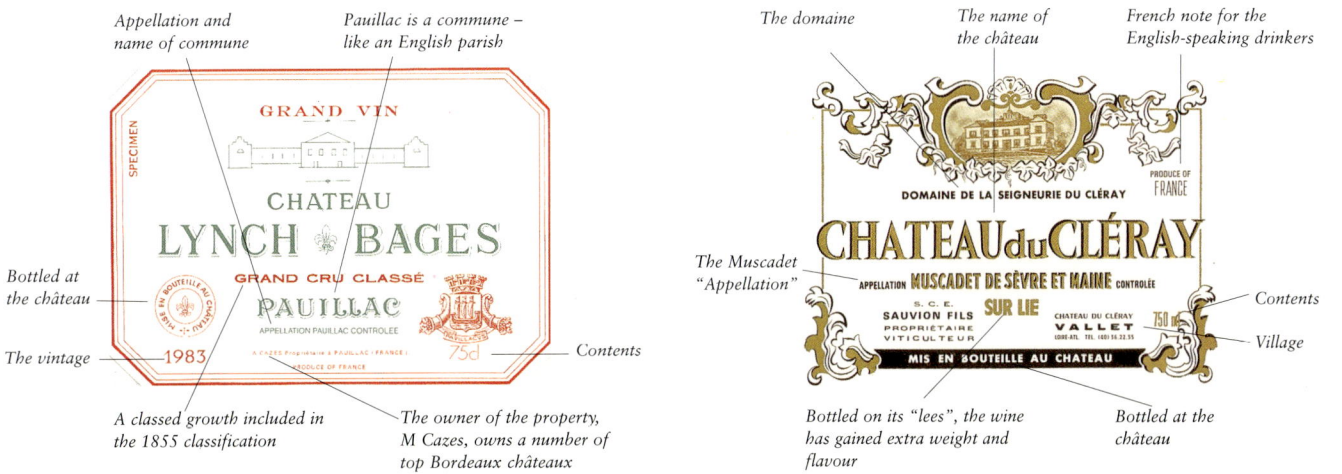

Appellation and name of commune

Pauillac is a commune – like an English parish

Bottled at the château

The vintage

A classed growth included in the 1855 classification

The owner of the property, M Cazes, owns a number of top Bordeaux châteaux

Contents

The domaine

The name of the château

French note for the English-speaking drinkers

The Muscadet "Appellation"

Bottled on its "lees", the wine has gained extra weight and flavour

Contents

Village

Bottled at the château

Reading the Label

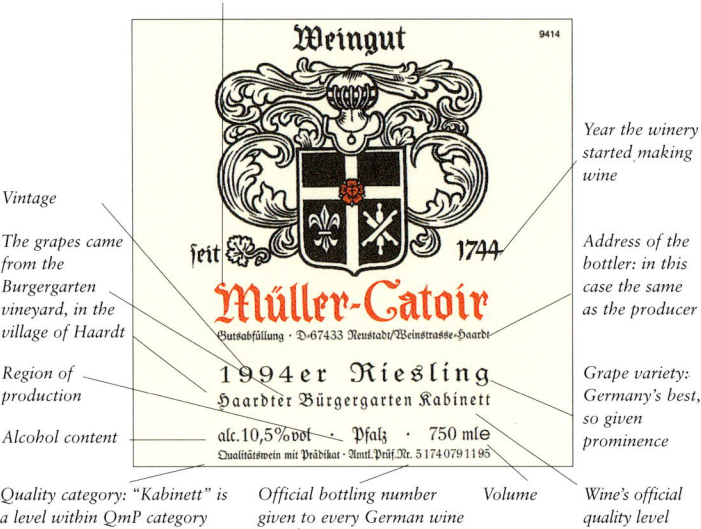

Name of the producer. Many German labels are addicted to Gothic lettering which makes few concessions to readability for non-Germans

Year the winery started making wine

Vintage

The grapes came from the Burgergarten vineyard, in the village of Haardt

Address of the bottler: in this case the same as the producer

Region of production

Grape variety: Germany's best, so given prominence

Alcohol content

Quality category: "Kabinett" is a level within QmP category

Official bottling number given to every German wine

Volume

Wine's official quality level

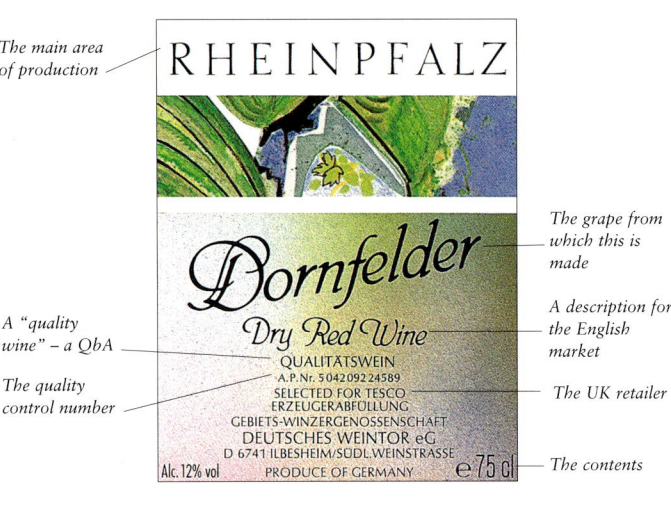

The main area of production

A "quality wine" – a QbA

The quality control number

The grape from which this is made

A description for the English market

The UK retailer

The contents

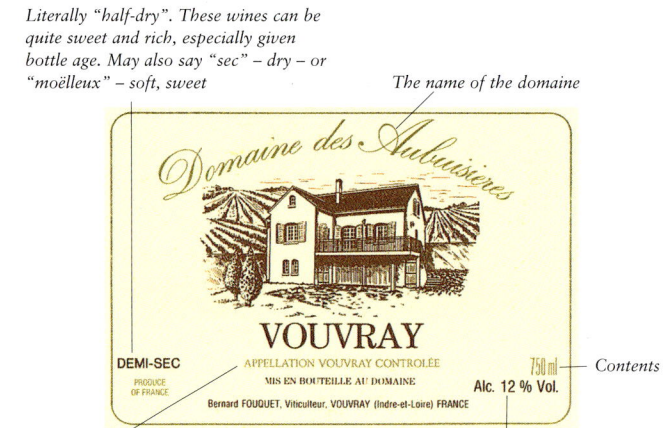

Literally "half-dry". These wines can be quite sweet and rich, especially given bottle age. May also say "sec" – dry – or "moëlleux" – soft, sweet

The name of the domaine

Contents

"Appellation"

Alcoholic strength

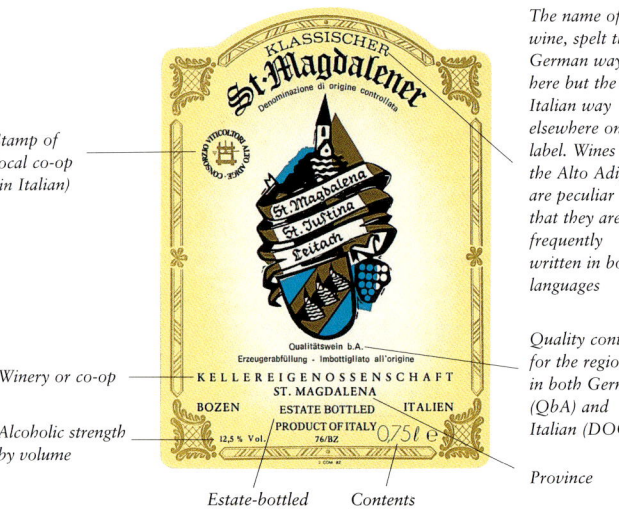

The name of the wine, spelt the German way here but the Italian way elsewhere on the label. Wines from the Alto Adige are peculiar in that they are frequently written in both languages

Stamp of local co-op (in Italian)

Winery or co-op

Alcoholic strength by volume

Estate-bottled

Contents

Quality control for the region, in both German (QbA) and Italian (DOC)

Province

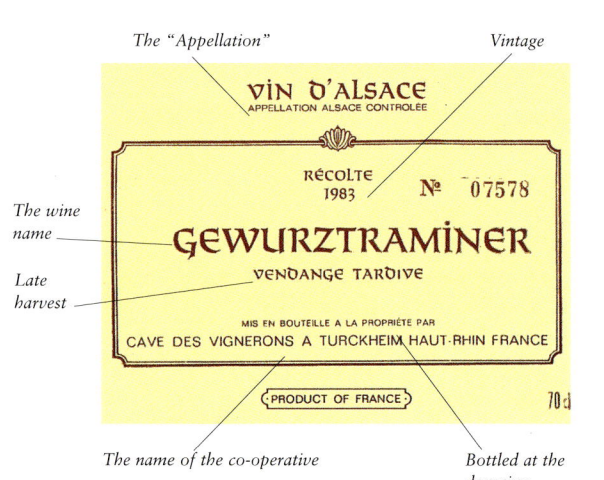

The "Appellation"

Vintage

The wine name

Late harvest

The name of the co-operative

Bottled at the domaine

54

Reading the Label

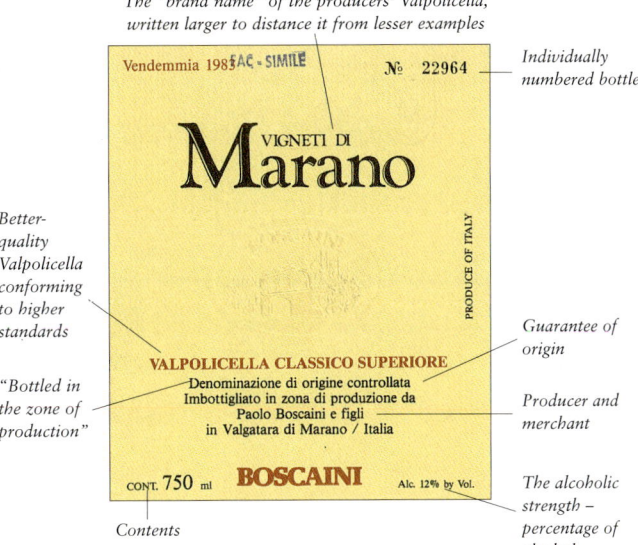

The "brand name" of the producers' Valpolicella, written larger to distance it from lesser examples — **Vigneti di Marano**

Individually numbered bottle — No. 22964

Better-quality Valpolicella conforming to higher standards — Valpolicella Classico Superiore

Guarantee of origin — Denominazione di origine controllata

"Bottled in the zone of production" — Imbottigliato in zona di produzione

Producer and merchant — Paolo Boscaini e figli in Valgatara di Marano / Italia

Contents — 750 ml

The alcoholic strength – percentage of alcohol — Alc. 12% by Vol.

By volume: many Barolos are notable for their high strength of alcohol — Alc. 14% by Vol.

The name of the wine, registered as a trademark — Monprivato

Contents — 750 ml

The number of bottles, magnums and double magnums produced in this vintage — 13148 Albeise – 66 Magnum – 30 Grandi Albeise

Individual bottle number — No. 11553

The abbreviation for the official EU term, "Vin de Qualité Produit Dans une Région Delimitée" — VQPRD

Estate-bottled by grower — Imbottigliato all'origine dal viticoltore Mauro Mascarello a Monchiero

Denominazione de Origine Controllata e Garantita; the highest Italian quality designation

Semi-sweet — Amabile

DOC quality. Semi-sparkling "natural fermentation" — Vino Frizzante a fermentazione naturale

Brand name (registered) — Cavicchioli

Co-op bottled — Imbottigliato nelle cantine

Contents — 75 cl.e

Town of co-op — San Prospero (MO)

Alcohol content: 8 per cent. The 3 per cent refers to the potential alcohol of the wine's residual sugar — 8 + 3% VOL.

The alcoholic strength, traditional sherries have 15.5 to 17 per cent alcohol — 17% VOL.

Contents — 70 cl.e

Producer — Diez Hermanos

Spanish name — Jerez

English name — Sherry

Style (dry) — DRY

Term used for export to denote fine quality fino — Palma FINO

Shipper and bottler — Blandy's

Brand name — Duke of Clarence

Name of the wine, made on the island of Madeira — Madeira

Style (grape variety) — Rich Malmsey

Producer — Produced by Blandys Madeiras Lda, Madeira

Contents — 70 cl.

Reading the Label

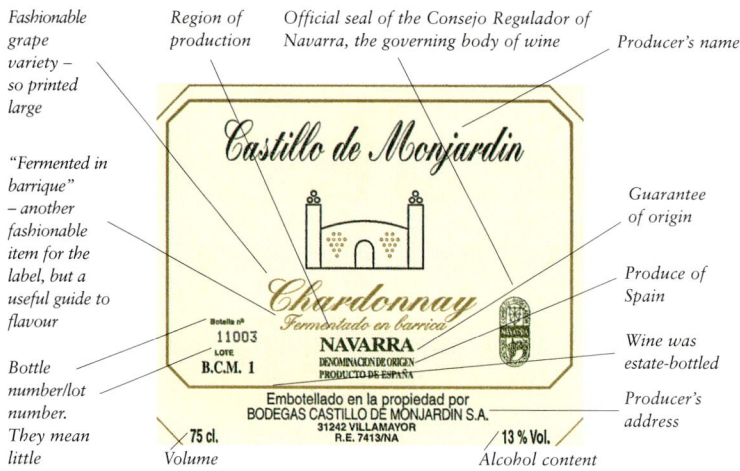

- Fashionable grape variety – so printed large
- Region of production
- Official seal of the Consejo Regulador of Navarra, the governing body of wine
- Producer's name
- "Fermented in barrique" – another fashionable item for the label, but a useful guide to flavour
- Guarantee of origin
- Produce of Spain
- Wine was estate-bottled
- Bottle number/lot number. They mean little
- Producer's address
- Volume
- Alcohol content

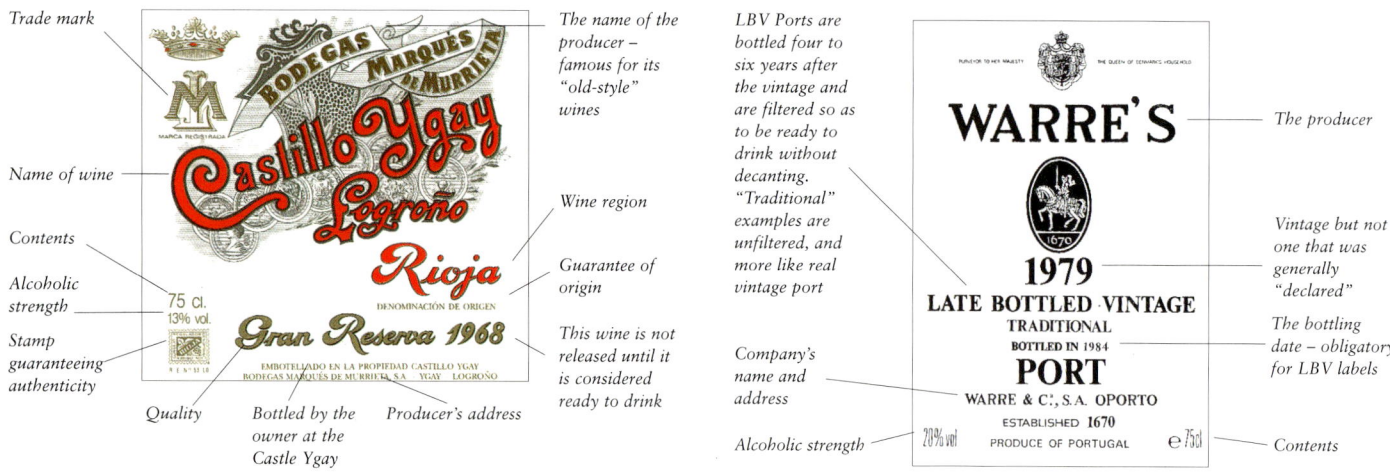

- Trade mark
- Name of wine
- Contents
- Alcoholic strength
- Stamp guaranteeing authenticity
- Quality
- Bottled by the owner at the Castle Ygay
- Producer's address
- The name of the producer – famous for its "old-style" wines
- Wine region
- Guarantee of origin
- This wine is not released until it is considered ready to drink
- LBV Ports are bottled four to six years after the vintage and are filtered so as to be ready to drink without decanting. "Traditional" examples are unfiltered, and more like real vintage port
- Company's name and address
- Alcoholic strength
- The producer
- Vintage but not one that was generally "declared"
- The bottling date – obligatory for LBV labels
- Contents

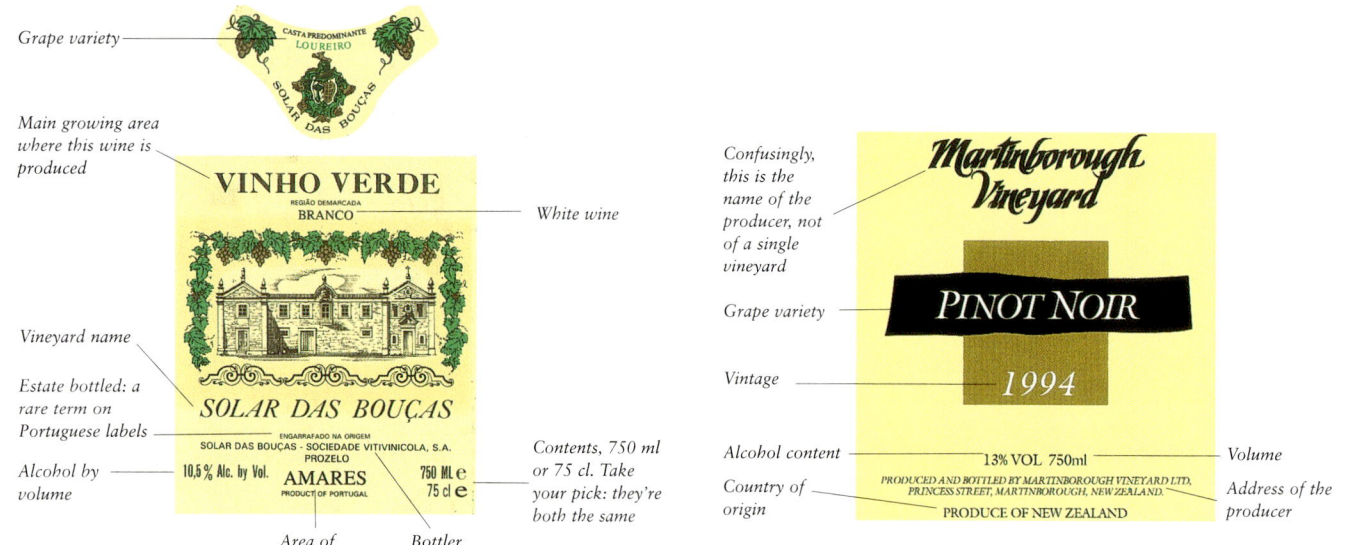

- Grape variety
- Main growing area where this wine is produced
- Vineyard name
- Estate bottled: a rare term on Portuguese labels
- Alcohol by volume
- White wine
- Area of production
- Bottler
- Contents, 750 ml or 75 cl. Take your pick: they're both the same
- Confusingly, this is the name of the producer, not of a single vineyard
- Grape variety
- Vintage
- Alcohol content
- Country of origin
- Volume
- Address of the producer

Reading the Label

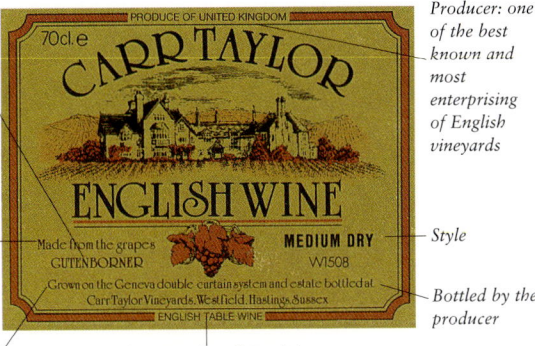

Grape variety: a German cross typical of varieties grown in England

Wine made from fresh English grapes – never, never confuse this with "British wine" made from imported grape concentrate

The Geneva double curtain is a method of vine-training developed in America

Producer: one of the best known and most enterprising of English vineyards

Style

Bottled by the producer

Under EU rules, all English wine regardless of quality is designated as "table wine", though many deserve better

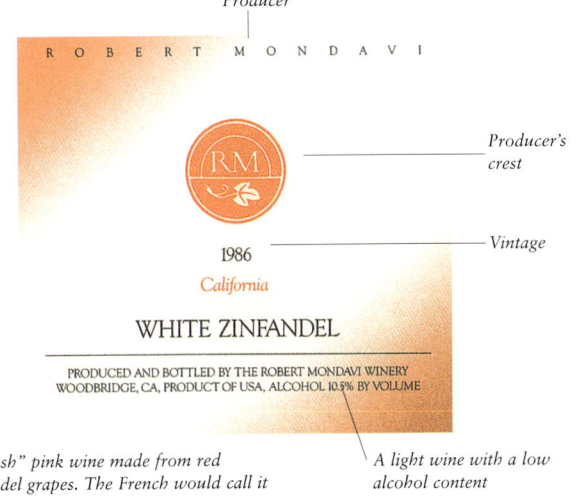

Producer

Producer's crest

Vintage

A "blush" pink wine made from red Zinfandel grapes. The French would call it rosé

A light wine with a low alcohol content

Name of the producer. Coonawarra is is one the finest vineyard areas in Australia, but here it forms part of a company name

Added to Wynn's labels to mark their centenary in 1991

Vintage

Address

Alcohol content

Grape variety

Volume

Address of the British importer

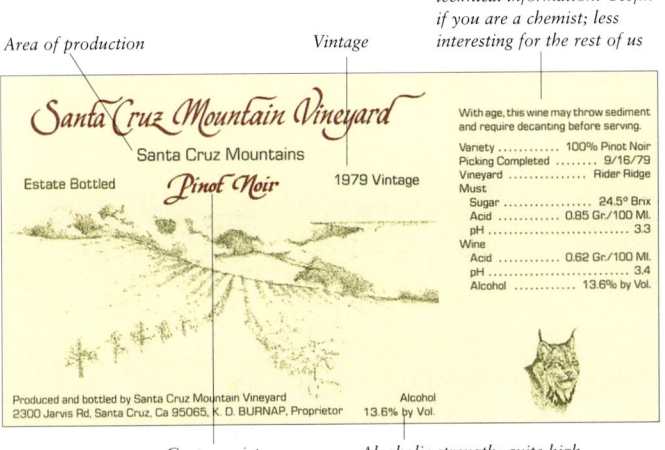

Area of production

Vintage

Many "New-World" wines go in for this complex level of technical information. Useful if you are a chemist; less interesting for the rest of us

Grape variety

Alcoholic strength: quite high

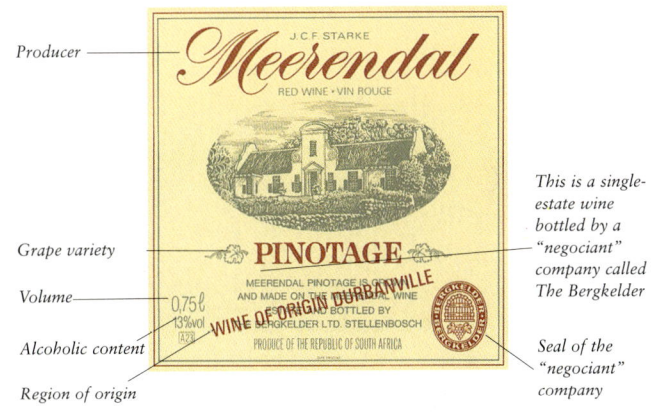

Producer

Grape variety

Volume

Alcoholic content

Region of origin

This is a single-estate wine bottled by a "negociant" company called The Bergkelder

Seal of the "negociant" company

57

Tasting

There are few more pretentious sights than a restaurant diner taking his time pompously sniffing, sipping and considering a wine while his embarrassed guests pause in their conversation so as not to jeopardize his (yes, it is almost always a man) concentration. Especially when it transpires that the object of all this attention is the house red. There are, of course, occasions when it is appropriate to examine a wine as if it were a rare manuscript, but these are rare. The best way to spot the real wine expert is to look for the person who simply takes a brief sniff of the glass he is offered before nodding his approval.

But why go through the rigmarole of tasting in the first place? Well, there are four basic reasons for doing so:

- to see if there is anything wrong with it;
- to decide whether or not you like it;
- to judge whether it is a good example of its type;
- to guess its identity and vintage in a "blind" tasting.

Most people are only usually concerned with the first two of these. But the third can be as important to the wine-drinker as it is, say, to a wine-merchant or restaurateur. Is the wine a "good buy"? And does it taste as it should? Of

Comparing the colour of two reds at a wine tasting.

course, wines that are atypical of their style or region can be delicious, too, but if that glass of pleasant "Sancerre" is actually filled with a blend of heaven-knows-what from heaven-knows-where, it should have cost you a lot less money. A little knowledge and practice will enable you to recognize and memorize styles and flavours.

Being able to tell a Rioja from a claret when you have both in front of you, however, is far easier than guessing the precise identity and age of a single glass of wine "blind". This is the skill professional tasters use to help them assess each wine they encounter quite simply on its own merits.

But is this a gift with which they are born? Or a party trick anyone can learn? The answer to both questions is yes. Just as there are children who seem to have a natural affinity for a tennis racket or a piano keyboard, there are unquestionably men and women who are instinctively better at remembering the things they see and taste. But, given a little effort, we can all be taught to pick out a tune, to sketch a landscape or to get the ball back over the net. And we can all learn to hold our own in a blind tasting.

The key to identifying a wine lies in its combination of visual, smell and taste "triggers" – the ones you remember from the last time you tasted it. You are using your memory just as you would to recognize a Rolling Stones song from the first Keith Richards guitar chord or a Strauss waltz by its distinctive lilt, orchestration and harmonies.

These triggers often work unconsciously – but they do rely on the information having been stored in the first place. So concentrate for a moment or two on every glass of wine you drink. Will you recognize it next time you taste it?

COLOUR

First of all, scrutinize the colour, holding the wine, if possible, against a well-lit white surface. Since white wines tend to darken as they age, paleness will suggest youthfulness. A pale wine, perhaps with greenish glints, will be light in body and may well be from a cool climate – grapes grown in hot climates such as Australia or California have deeper pigmentation and so impart more colour to the fermenting juice. A wine with lots of yellow-tinged colour could be a recent vintage from a warm climate, or it might be a moderately mature wine with long barrel-ageing such as an old-style Rioja. Alternatively, fine old Chardonnays darken when in an advanced state of maturity, while dessert wines often look golden.

Smelling a wine should tell you if there's anything wrong with it.

With red wines, the general colour depends on where the grapes are from, regardless of age. So look at the rim: an intense purple is indicative of a young full-bodied wine, perhaps from the very warm Rhône, while a fresh, ruby colour is characteristic of a lighter wine and might suggest, for example, a Beaujolais. A chestnut rim suggests a more mature wine but beware – wines mature at different rates. It could be a relatively young Rioja that has had long barrel-ageing, or a young wine from a poor vintage near the end of its foreshortened life. Or it could be a very mellow Burgundy or claret.

Then, swirl the wine in the glass (the increased air contact makes the wine release more of its aromas), and take a big sniff.

SMELL

The smell of a wine is its taste. Just as you can tell that a piece of meat is "off" by sniffing it, you can also use your nose to tell you whether there is anything wrong with a wine. On the other hand, there are some perfectly normal wine smells which you simply may not like. Sancerre is often said to smell of cat's pee; Australian Shiraz of "sweaty saddle"; and old red Burgundy, "farmyardy". None of these

The Language of Wine-Tasting

Acetic Vinegary – the wine has been "got at" by bacteria.
Acidity – The essential natural component which gives wine freshness and zing and prevents it from cloying.
Aggressive – Over-tannic or over-acidic.
Alcoholic – Over-alcoholic wine tastes "hot", burns the palate.
Almond – Bitter almond can denote Tocai from Italy.
Aniseed – Found in red Burgundy and – to a lesser extent – Bordeaux and some Northern Italian whites.
Apple – A smell often found in young white wines, from the Bramley freshness of Vinho Verde, young Loire, Chardonnay and English wines, through to the ripe Cox's of more mature white Burgundies, Champagne and some white Bordeaux. Stewed or baked apple can be a sure sign of Riesling. Unripe apple is often a sign that a wine has not undergone its malolactic fermentation.
Apricot – Common in the white Rhônes of Condrieu and Château-Grillet and other examples of the Viognier grape, and in wine from *botrytis*-affected grapes.
Aromatic – Often associated with wines made from grapes such as the Gewürztraminer and Muscat.
Artificial also **Contrived, Confected** – Used to describe wines whose taste appears to have been created chemically.
Attack – The quality in a wine which makes you sit up and take notice.
Austere – A wine difficult to approach, with fruit not obvious. Wait for the flavour to open out in the mouth.
Backward – Not as developed as its age would lead you to expect.
Bad eggs – Presence of hydrogen sulphide, usually a result of faulty cellaring or winemaking.
Baked – Like stewed fruits, probably from an over-warm vintage.
Balance – A balanced wine has its fruitiness, acidity, alcohol and tannin (for reds) in pleasant harmony.
Banana – A smell usually associated with young wine, fermented at low temperatures and – in the case of reds – in an oxygen-free environment. A sign of macération carbonique.
Beefy – Big, hearty, meaty wine.
Beeswing – A skin which forms on certain old ports, leaving a characteristic residue in the glass.

Big – Mouth-filling, full-flavoured, possibly strongly alcoholic.
Biscuity – Often used to describe the bouquet of Champagne.
Bite – High acidity, good in young wine.
Blackcurrant – Found in Cabernet Sauvignon and Pinot Noir wines. See also *Cassis*.
Blowsy – Exaggeratedly fruity, lacking bite.
Body – A full-bodied wine fills the mouth with flavour.
Bottle-sick – Newly bottled wines may take some time (sometimes months) to recover from the shock of air-contact and sulphuring at bottling.
Bottle stink – Wines which have just been opened may have a musty smell – bottle stink – which disappears in the glass.
Bouquet – Smell.
Brettanomyces/"Brett" – A "mousey" bacterial fault about which Californians are often fanatical, finding it almost everywhere they taste, from Bordeaux to the Barossa Valley. Tasters from other countries seem far less sensitive to it.
Butter – A richness of aroma and texture found in mature Chardonnay, and/or evidence of malolactic fermentation.
Caramel – A buttery toffee smell in wines like Madeira.
Cassis – Literally, blackcurrant; used when the sensation is of an intense, heady syrup rather than the fresh fruit.
Cat's pee – The pungent smell of Sauvignon Blanc and Müller-Thurgau.
Cedar – An aroma of maturing claret.
Chaptalized – Chaptalization is the process of adding sugar to fermenting must to increase the alcoholic strength. If overdone, a wine tastes "hot".
Cherry – A characteristic of Beaujolais – particularly Morgon.
Chocolate – For some people, a sure sign of the Pinot Noir grape.
Cigar-box – See *cedar*.
Closed – Has yet to show its quality.
Cloudy – A sign of a faulty wine.
Cloying – A sickly taste, sweetness without acidity.
Clumsy – An unbalanced wine.
Coffee – Special characteristic of old, great Burgundy, though I also find it in some great claret such as Mouton Rothschild.
Commercial – Light, drinkable, undemanding wine.
Complex – Having a diverse, well-blended mixture of smells and flavours.

Cooked – A "warm", stewed-fruit flavour – may suggest over-warm fermentation or the use of grape concentrate.
Corked – A wine spoiled by a bad cork has a musty smell and flavour.
Crisp – Fresh, lively, with good acidity.
Crust – Deposit thrown by a mature port.
Depth – Wine with depth fills the mouth with lingering flavour.
Dirty – Badly made wine can taste unclean.
Dirty socks – Cheesy sourness accompanying badly made white wine.
Dry – Having no obvious sweetness.
Dried out – A wine which has lost its fruit as it has aged.
Dumb – No apparent smell.
Dusty – Sometimes used to describe tannic Bordeaux – literally the "dusty" smell of an attic.
Earthy – Not as unpleasant as it sounds – an "earthy" flavour can characterize certain fine Burgundy.
Eggy – Carelessly handled sulphur can produce an eggy smell.
Elegant – Restrained, classy.
Esters – Sweet-smelling, often fruity compounds.
Eucalyptus – A flavour and smell often found in Cabernet Sauvignon from Australia, Californian Cabernet Sauvignon (Martha's Vineyard) and, though more rarely, in Bordeaux (e.g. Château Latour).
Extract – The concentration of the grape's flavours in a wine.
Farmyard – A characteristic of Burgundian Pinot Noir.
Fat – Used to describe mouth-filling wines, especially Chardonnay and white wines from the Rhône and Alsace.
Finesse – Understated, classy.
Finish – How a wine's flavour ends in the mouth. Can be "long" or "short".
Flabby – Lacking balancing acidity.
Flat – Short of acidity and fruit.
Flinty/gunflint – "Stonily" crisp, used of whites; Pouilly-Fumé, for example.
Flor – A yeast film which grows on top of the fermenting must of fino sherry.
Forward – A precocious wine showing its qualities earlier than expected.
Foxy – A peculiar "wild" smell found in labrusca grapes and wine in the USA.
Gamey – Used of mature Burgundy, Rhône Syrah and Australian Shiraz. It's a smell that combines meat and spice.

Tasting

Generous – Big, mouth-filling, round.
Geraniums – The smell of the leaves of this flower indicates the presence of an unwelcome micro-organism formed during fermentation.
Glycerine – The "fatty" constituent in some wines, making them taste richer – the "legs" which flow down the inside of the glass.
Gooseberry – The smell of Sauvignon, especially Loire and New Zealand.
Grapey – It's surprising how rare this flavour is: Muscat and Riesling are often grapey; so is good Beaujolais.
Grassy – "Green" smell of young wine, especially Sauvignon Blanc and Cabernet Franc.
Green pepper – Can be the sign of Cabernet Sauvignon – in Bordeaux, or indeed anywhere else.
Grip – Firm wine has "grip". Essential to some styles.
Gris – Very pale pink.
Hazelnut – Along with toasted almonds, can indicate rich maturing Chardonnay.
Herbaceous – Think of a cross between grass and flowers – "planty".
Herby – Some wines from the south-west of France, as well as from Italy, can smell positively herby – almost like a pizza, fresh from the grill.
Hollow – Lacking depth and roundness.
Honey – An obvious description for most of the great sweet white wines of the world, but also a characteristic – in its richness rather than its sweetness – of some mature white Burgundy and much Chenin Blanc from the Loire.
Hot – Used to describe over-chaptalized, over-alcoholic wine.
Iodine – A smell and taste sometimes encountered in wines made from grapes grown close to the sea.
Jammy – A jammy fruit smell often signifies red wines from hot countries.
Lanolin – Some white wines have an oily softness reminiscent of lanolin.
Legs – The visible evidence of glycerine in a wine, these are the "tears" that run down the glass's side after swirling.
Lemon – Young whites may display a lemony freshness.
Length – The time the flavour stays in the mouth.
Liquorice – Encountered in all sorts of wine – from claret and port to Burgundy.
Lychees – Common in wines made from the Gewürztraminer grape.
Maderized – The rancio character of heat-induced oxidation.
Malic acid – The component of wine converted by malolactic fermentation into softer lactic acid. Smells like green apples in young white wines.
Meaty – A wine to get your teeth into.
Mellow – Soft and mature.
Mercaptans – A smell of rotten eggs or burnt rubber, stemming from the mishandling of sulphur dioxide.
Metallic – Taste/smell arising from the use of poor equipment.
Mint – Often found in Cabernet Sauvignons.
Mouldy – Taste/smell arising from rotten grapes, poor wine-making or a bad cork.
Mouth-puckering – Young, tannic or over-acidic wine has this effect.
Mulberry – The ripe berry flavour of some Pomerol.
Mushroom – Can indicate quality reds but also a wine past its prime.
Nose – The smell of a wine.
Nutty – Especially of Chardonnay and sherry.
Oaky – In moderation, pleasant, like vanilla. Especially New-World wines and Rioja.
Old socks (clean) – A promising sign of young white Burgundy, particularly Chablis.
Oxidized – If a table wine looks and smells of sherry, it's oxidized – a diagnosis confirmed by its colour: brown for red wines, deep yellow for whites.
Palate – The flavour, and what you taste it with.
Pear drops – Smell which is usually the mark of a very young wine.
Pepper – Black, not green: the sign of the Grenache or Syrah in the Rhône.
Pétillant – Slight sparkle or spritz.
Petrol – A desirable aroma of mature Riesling.
Pine – Aroma found in Retsina.
Plum – Especially clarets, Rioja and Burgundy.
Quaffing, quaffable – Everyday wine, usually soft, fruity and undemanding.
Rancio – Rich, distinctive flavour of certain wines, particularly southern French *vins doux naturels* stored in barrels exposed to heat.
Raspberry – Aroma associated with Syrah, Gamay and much Pinot Noir.
Residual sugar – The natural grape sugar left in a wine which has not been fermented into alcohol.
Ripe – Grapes were fully ripe when picked.
Robust – Solid, full-bodied.
Rose – Often the choicest clarets, some cru Beaujolais and Côte de Beaune.
Rough – Unbalanced and coarse.
Round – Smooth and harmonious.
Rubber – Some wines can smell rubbery, though not unpleasant. This is an aroma often associated with red wines from South Africa, Beaujolais, Californian Zinfandel and American Pinot Noir.
Salt – A salty tang, almost like iodine, associated with Manzanilla sherry.
Sediment – Precipitation of tannins in red wine due to ageing.
Short – Wine with a short finish.
Silky – Exceptionally smooth.
Smoke – The most famous smoky wine is Pouilly Blanc Fumé, made from the Sauvignon Blanc. Alsace Tokay-Pinot Gris, Corsican rosés, some Bordeaux, and Syrah from the Rhône may also be smoky.
Spicy – Wines made from grapes such as the Syrah, Grenache and Zinfandel can be positively spicy. Also whites from the Gewürztraminer, Albariño, Arneis, Viognier.
Spritz – Slight sparkle. Or faint fizz. Similar to *pétillant*.
Stalky or Stemmy – The flavour of the grape stem rather than of the juice.
Steely – Attractively crisp, with a firm backbone of acidity.
Strawberry – The taste of some Gamay, Pinot Noir and Rioja.
Structure – Wine with good structure has, or will have, all its elements in harmony.
Sulphur – The antiseptic used to protect wine from bacteria. Its throat-tickling aroma should disappear after the wine has been swirled in the glass for a moment, or left in the open bottle for a while. Often, however, it is "locked in" and prevents the wine from ever being pleasant.
Tannin – The mouth-puckering ingredient in red wine. Softens with age.
Tobacco – Like cigar-box, found in oak-aged reds, especially clarets.
Toffee – Often indicates the presence of the Merlot grape in red Bordeaux.
Truffles – Mushroom and vegetal aromas, especially in red wines.
Vanilla – Aroma of wines matured in American oak casks; also white Burgundy and oak-aged Rioja.
Vegetal – Earthy, wet-leaf smell; cabbagey, often of big Italian red wines.
Violets – Floral red Burgundies and Chiantis can smell intensely of violets.
Volatile – In an unstable – volatile – wine, acids evaporate from the surface giving vinegary, sometimes "greasy" smells.
Yeast – Like newly baked bread; smell found in Champagne, Muscadet sur lie and some nuttily rich white wines.

FAULTS

One of the greatest areas of confusion when tasting and drinking wine is whether "it's supposed to taste like this". In other words, is it worth sending the bottle back and requesting another?

There are two kinds of faulty wine: the ones which have been badly made – in which case the whole vat or barrel will be equally unpleasant – and the odd bottle which has been mistreated or "got at" by bacteria. When in doubt, wine experts generally give the wine-maker the benefit of the doubt by calling for a replacement; sometimes it is perfect and sometimes it as nasty or nastier than the stuff it is replacing.

To help you discern faults for yourself, though, the following are some you might find.

Appearance
A wine which looks cloudy when carefully poured from a bottle which has been allowed to stand for a few hours is probably faulty, though it may taste fine. Carelessly decanted wines and ones which have been shaken up before serving may also look cloudy of course.

Do not worry about the fine, dark film which is sometimes found within bottles of Australian red – it is simply the deposit – nor about the white crystals encountered at the bottom of some whites. Known as "wine diamonds" in Germany, these are a natural tartrate deposit which would be far more commonplace if producers did not generally chill their white wines to precipitate them before bottling.

Any wine which looks brown, unless you know it to be of an advanced age, is probably past its sell-by date or has been oxidized by poor handling.

Smell
If the stuff in your glass smells like sherry and does not describe itself as sherry or one of the rare sherry-like wines described on p. 43, it is oxidized. This could be caused by age, a leaky cork or storage in a warm place. Unless you suspect age to be the culprit, ask for a replacement. If it smells vinegary, this again could be a case of a poor bottle, though there's a significant chance that careless wine-making could be responsible. Mustiness is another frequent problem. But before complaining, give the wine a chance to breathe; sometimes what older wine buffs used to call "bottle stink" will disappear after a few minutes' exposure to the air. If the symptoms persist, you may have a wine which was matured in dirty wooden casks or one which is "corked".

This last condition, often wrongly diagnosed on the basis of a few harmless crumbs of cork floating on the surface of the wine – the result of the cork breaking apart as it is pulled from the bottle – is caused by generally invisible, but sadly quite prevalent, types of mould. Corked bottles are recognizable from a smell which resembles a combination of stale dried mushrooms and damp cellars which tends to intensify the longer the bottle is open. Most winemakers admit that as many as one in 12 corks may be more or less affected by this mould. Buying a pricey wine does little to lengthen the odds against getting a bad bottle – though there is little question that "agglomerate" corks, made from tiny chips glued together and used almost exclusively for cheap wines, seem particularly subject to mouldy smells and flavours.

Ironically, research has shown that the most efficient way to seal a wine bottle would be with a screwcap, but since few wine buffs are ready to unscrew a bottle of Mouton Rothschild, go-ahead producers in California and Chile and supermarkets in Britain have instead switched to recently developed polypropylene corks.

Another fault you may encounter is the presence of some form of sulphur. Cough-inducing sulphur dioxide is common in recently bottled wines and most particularly sweet ones from the traditional areas of Europe (New-World wine-makers are less tolerant of it), while a gluey or a manure-like smell reveals unwelcome sulphur compounds in the wine. One way to check your diagnosis of these is to drop a copper coin into the glass and leave it in contact with the wine for a few minutes. Often, the copper will clean up the problem. Unfortunately, a bottle with one of these sulphur-related conditions is probably typical of a whole batch.

are odours many people find pleasant as such, but they can be likened (hopefully not too exactly) to characteristic traits of an old friend: essential facets of his or her personality.

The majority of good wines, however, display a wonderfully diverse collection of pleasant smells. Few of these appear to have any direct relation to grapes – indeed, it's astonishing how this single fruit, grown and vinified in different ways, manages to produce not only so many aromas, but in blends of a complexity and success a perfumier would be hard-pressed to match.

And just as a perfumier divides scents into groups, so wine-smells fall into categories – fruity, floral, spicy, vegetal, earthy and woody. So when you sniff a wine and find apricot where someone else finds plum, don't worry, neither of you is wrong; you're both choosing nuances you recognize from the same "fruity" group. And if you think that a wine smells of something truly bizarre – Chablis of wet wool, for instance – take note of it; it's your personal key to picking out Chablis "blind" next time.

The glossary of tasting terms on pages 60–61 gives you an indication of smells often associated with particular wines.

For some reason, women are often better at this aspect of wine-tasting than men. The female nostril may well naturally be more sensitive than the male – after all, women choose perfume much more carefully than most men select their aftershave – or it may be that they are simply more

The serious business of tasting all those wines!

used to paying attention to the way things smell.

The key to being able to identify wines by their smell lies in constructing your own smell vocabulary, which can be built up by practising on the aromas you encounter every day. Do Golden Delicious apples smell the same as Cox's? Compare the smell of new and old leather…

A final point: what if a wine doesn't appear to smell of anything at all? Well, it's either a very boring wine, or one that is very reluctant to release its bouquet; professional tasters will simply describe it as a "dumb nose" and move on to the taste in order to find out why.

TASTE

Take a generous sip – and roll it around in your mouth. When wine-tasters suck in air through their teeth and make slurping noises, they're aerating the wine in their mouth just as they swirl it in the glass before sniffing.

What your mouth (your "palate") is going to tell you about the wine is not its flavour – the flavours you "taste" in your mouth are actually being "smelt" in your nasal cavity above – but its structure; that is, its texture (rough or smooth), its "body" (light or full), and its "balance" – the happy or unhappy combination of elements such as sweetness, acidity, fruit, alcohol and, in red wine, tannin.

The first question to ask yourself when tasting any wine is "does it taste good?" If it does, it's a fairly good indication that it has been well made. Of course, if you absolutely detest sweet wine, the finest Sauternes or Trockenbeerenauslese isn't going to give you much pleasure. Even so, most people can give a fair judgement on whether a piece of music is played well or not, even if it isn't to their taste.

But just as the trio can drown the singer's voice, the essential quality of any good wine – cheap or expensive – is its balance. A young wine can appear to be unbalanced, most commonly because high acidity or tannin are obscuring the flavour of the fruit. When they are first made, red wines which have been built to last can be very tannic. Experienced tasters should be able to discern future quality nevertheless, but even they can get it wrong sometimes. A very tannic, apparently fruitless, young wine can develop

Tasting

The ideal job? Tasting wine at a quality control centre.

into a rich and complex mature one, but the fruit has to be in there somewhere.

Young white wines can taste very acidic but, similarly, it is this acidity which will enable them to age – provided they are of a style which needs maturity. White wines intended to be drunk young – Muscadet, Frascati, Vinho Verde – need acidity to give them freshness, but in these cases that tang must be balanced by fruit. If your bottle tastes tart and fruitless, you simply have an inferior example which is unlikely to improve.

No wine should ever taste sharp or bitter – although some Italian whites seem to be resolutely sour. If you think a wine tastes of vinegar, it may well have been got at by "acetobacters" – vinegar bacteria. On the other hand, wines which seem flabby are probably suffering from too little acidity, often the result of the grapes having been carelessly handled in a warm climate.

Inexperienced tasters often imagine that poor wine tends to be acidic and vinegary; generally though, far too many poor wines are simply dull and inoffensive, tasting of nothing at all. These should not, however, be confused with some good wines which are reticent with their flavours, just as they were "dumb" on the nose – these are described as "closed", needing more time in bottle, or a little contact with oxygen to "bring them out". How do you tell the difference? It's like guessing whether a shy person has anything to say. Does there seem to be something worth digging out? If so, leave the wine in the glass for a while and come back to it.

Finally, the "finish". Tasters often describe wines as "long" or "short" – meaning that the wine's flavour either lingers pleasantly in the mouth after the wine is swallowed, or seems rapidly to melt away. If a wine is slightly faulty or off-balance, you may find that it is the flawed or excessive element that comes out most strongly on the finish – the dry-mouthed sensation created by high tannins or too much oak, for example.

So, your tasting armoury is complete. Your smell and taste "triggers" will have helped you to make a guess at the wine's origin and grape variety; the colour, its age; qualities of its structure may help to verify both, and tell you whether the wine is too young, too old, or ready to drink. If all (or nearly all) of these elements are pleasing and, essentially, they come together to give balance, you have a good wine.

WHAT MAKES WINE GREAT

But what makes a good wine "great" and worth the praise it gets and the price it commands? How do experts compare different wines to decide which is the best – and the best value? Judging the quality of a wine is little different from assessing the quality of any other human creation – from a garden or a meal to a novel or a symphony. Well, everything that makes it good must be there in spades – but then one moves on into less easily definable territory. Tasters may use words like "classy" or "elegant" to describe a fine wine. A great wine's key characteristic is complexity – the perception of a host of nuances and flavours, perfectly interwoven, to which one wants to return again and again.

To place wines on a scale of greatness, professional wine tasters – winemakers, consultants, merchants and critics for the most part – tend to give wines marks. Traditionally, the number earned was often out of 20, a possible total which was broken down into – for example – three points for colour; five for the "nose"; seven for flavour and five for "overall" quality. Rating wines in this way is rather like ranking a film by giving points respectively to the acting, direction, camerawork, costumes and music. While this kind of precision suits some people, others like me, find it too restrictive. There are some wines which I simply feel deserve eight points – or 18.

Tasting

In any case, the whole business of giving wines points has been further complicated by the decision of the US wine guru Robert Parker and – subsequently – the *Wine Spectator* magazine, to mark wines out of 100, using a quirky American academic scale that starts at 50. Which, when you come to think of it, means that it isn't so much a 100-point scale as a 50-point one. In fact, the range is even narrower than that. Wines that rate less than 70 are barely drinkable and those with a mark of less than 80 are unlikely to excite a flicker of interest among readers and wine buyers in the USA who take these matters very seriously. The score these people are looking for is over 90. Indeed any wine lucky – or good – enough to score between 95 and 100 may well sell out overnight.

Apart from the points they may be given by critics, wines may also win medals and trophies in local, national and international competitions. As founder-chairman of the London International Wine Challenge competition (the biggest contest of its kind in the world, with over 8,500 entries) and of International Wine Challenges in Shanghai, Beijing, Singapore, Hong Kong and Tokyo, I naturally believe in the validity of these competitions, but I also readily concede that a blind tasting is a far from perfect way to assess a wine. There are all sorts of great subtle wines that pale by comparison when sampled briefly alongside more "showy" efforts in a competition, but really come

TRAINING YOUR TASTEBUDS

Taste buds are like muscles; so I've devised a few exercises – comparative tastings – with which to keep them in trim.

- **Fruity reds** Taste a range of blackcurrant Cabernet Sauvignons and Cabernet Francs, such as Bordeaux from the Médoc, red Loires such as Chinon or Bourgueil, and examples from Bulgaria, California and Australia. Then move onto the more cherry-like flavours of Beaujolais and good young Bardolino, and the raspberry taste of the Pinot Noir (from Burgundy, Sancerre, Alsace, Australia, Chile, California or Oregon).
- **Oaky wines** For this, you'll need a bottle or two of red Rioja con Crianza, a traditional white Rioja such as Monopole by CVNE, a Chardonnay from Australia (such as Rosemount's "Show Reserve") and a classy young Bordeaux (such as Château Lynch-Bages).
- **Spicy wines** The pepper of any Grenache from the southern Rhône (ideally Gigondas or Châteauneuf-du-Pape) can be compared with the deeper spice of the Syrah from further north (in Côte Rôtie or Hermitage) or Australia (where it's called the Shiraz), and with the tobaccoey flavours of good Nebbiolo from Barolo or Barbaresco.
- **Botrytis** Take a good Sauternes, a Beerenauslese from Germany or Austria and a "late-picked" Riesling from California or Australia – and look for that flavour of dried apricots.

into their own when they are drunk with appropriately chosen cuisine.

But assessing every one of the hundreds of thousands of wines produced every year with food is clearly impracticable, and there is no question that, while blind tastings may penalise some great bottles, in countries like Australia where they are taken seriously, they have also been hugely instrumental in raising the average quality of wine.

But what about price? Some competitions and critics take the cost of the bottle into account. Others – myself included – believe that there are too few controls on the way wine is sold to make this worthwhile. What happens, for example when, in reaction to demand, a retailer raises the price of a Gold medal red from £5 to £10? Would the tasters have given the wine that award if they had known the price tag it would eventually carry? Canny wine buyers calculate the value for money of any wine by setting its cost against the mark out of 100 or the medal it has won.

And they sensibly acknowledge that they aren't looking for "greatness" and complexity every time they have a glass of wine. A country church can be just as pleasing, in its own way, as St Peter's in Rome – perhaps even more so on a beautiful summer afternoon; musically, many of us would prefer, after a hard day, to unwind with Sondheim, not Stravinsky.

A blind tasting, where the labels are covered, are often instructive.

Cooking with Wine

"Go on – slosh in a bit more wine. Can't do any harm." Or can it? All sorts of nonsense has been spoken and written about cooking with wine. On the one hand, there are those wonderful old cookery books that recommend you use a priceless bottle of Chambertin for your coq au vin or boeuf bourguignon – because that's what the Duke of Burgundy's cook (who didn't have to pay for the stuff) would have used 600 years ago. On the other, there are the people who maintain that any wine that's too caustic to drink will be perfect for a sauce to serve with fillet steak.

Neither attitude makes sense. There is no point in boiling up a top-class red or white wine; nor, though, can you hope to get away with using just any old wine – any more than you can make a decent dish by casseroling any tough old chicken. First, ask yourself why (and how) you are going to use wine to prepare this dish. The answer is not as straightforward as you might imagine. There are some dishes in which the wine's essential role is as part of a marinade that will make tough meat tender; in others, such as coq au vin and that boeuf bourguignon, it will be the liquid in which the food is cooked. Often the wine will be added at the last minute to turn the juices and fats at the bottom of a roasting pan into a sauce; in a few cases, as in sherry trifle, it will simply taste of itself.

Give a thought, too, to the bottle you are going to serve with the meal. French traditionalists recommend that the two should be the same, or at least come from the same region; a more pragmatic approach would be to aim for wines of a similar style.

Be adventurous. After all, you could end up inventing a dish – in the way a long-forgotten Burgundian did when he or she first made the now-classic *oeufs en meurette*, by poaching eggs in the region's red wine.

Rules and hints

- Try to choose a style of wine that suits the particular dish you are cooking with as much care as you choose the food. A chicken does not taste like a duckling; a Beaujolais will not make the same kind of sauce as a Barolo.
- Don't cook with any wine you could not imagine drinking.
- Unless you are making a dish such as sherry trifle, in which you want the flavour of the alcohol to be apparent, don't pour in the wine right at the end of the

Wine is a staple in any good cook's store cupboard.

Many classic sauces are enhanced by the addition of wine.

cooking; cook the liquid for long enough for the alcohol to evaporate.
- Don't overdo it; adding another glassful of wine "for luck" can be too much of a good thing.
- You can make use of left-over wine and ensure that you always have some cooking wine to hand by preparing for yourself a "wine concentrate". All you have to do is simmer the wine (white or red) in a pan until its volume has been reduced by half. Prepared in this way, and frozen in ice-cube trays or stored in sterilized jam jars, the concentrate should keep almost indefinitely.

THE RIGHT WINE FOR THE RIGHT DISH

Champagne – When making dishes whose recipes call for Champagne (such as Champagne sorbet), don't make the mistake of substituting a cheap, basic sparkling wine. It wasn't the bubbles that the original cook was after, but the nutty, yeasty flavour. If you are not going to use Champagne, either go for a better-quality fizz from France, Australia, California or New Zealand or, perversely, you could try a high-quality Muscadet de Sèvre-et-Maine sur lie – these two words indicate that the wine has enjoyed the same yeasty contact as Champagne.

Dry white wine – Muscadet, Gros Plant and good dry, fairly neutral wines, such as young southern French *vins de pays* whose labels do not declare them to be Chardonnay, Sauvignon or whatever, basic Italian whites and modern-style white Rioja can be ideal for sauces to accompany shellfish. Richer wines, such as young white Burgundy and Bordeaux, Australian Sémillon (though only the lighter examples) and Alsace Pinot Blanc, can be better suited to white-meat dishes such as veal and pork. Sauvignon Blanc from New Zealand or the Loire can be used for these dishes or for poultry, as can dry Rieslings from Alsace or Germany and dry English wines. Another original idea is to sprinkle fruit salad with dry Riesling or Sauvignon just before serving.

Madeira – The sweeter styles of Madeira – Bual and Malmsey – are the ones to use for the classic sauce Madère, while the drier Sercial and Verdelho can be added to consommé. Sweet Madeira can also be poured over sorbet, substituted for Marsala in zabaglione or added to an apricot sauce for a fruit pie.

Marsala – When Marsala is specified in a recipe, as for example in zabaglione, it is almost always the sweet dolce style that is meant.

Medium white wine – Any recipe that simply calls for "medium white wine" is being very unhelpful; there is a huge difference in flavour between a cheap-and-nasty, semi-sweet "Rizling" from Eastern Europe and a demi-sec Vouvray, though both can fairly be described as "medium white". As a rule, go for the grapier (German Spätlese and QbA; Australian Rieslings) styles with any dish that includes grapes, and use demi-sec Loire Chenin Blancs and most examples of that grape from California for dishes with apple.

Muscat – Recipes that simply list Muscat probably mean a sweet, fortified version, such as Muscat de Frontignan or Beaumes de Venise.

Port – When French recipes require port, they can mean either cheap, basic tawny, or ruby – the two styles with which Gallic wine-drinkers are most familiar. Both can be used in variations of zabaglione.

Red wine – If the wine is going to be used as a marinade, choose one that has plenty of colour, flavour and tannin. Red Burgundy (with a few exceptions, such as Fixin) or Rioja are far less ideal for this purpose than more hard-edged, full-bodied wines, such as Barbera from Italy, Shiraz from Australia, Zinfandel from California, Douro from Portugal, or Corbières, Minervois or Cahors from France.

Similar styles of wine can be used when you are making sauces from the fat and juices that remain in the pan after you have roasted or sautéed almost any kind of meat. On the other hand, finer-flavoured wines such as Burgundies and Bordeaux are perfect for dishes that require the meat to be gently cooked in the wine.

Don't limit yourself to meat dishes with red wine; it can also be used with fruit to make all sorts of simple puddings. Fruit juice, sugar and wine can make a delicious sweet sauce, and various kinds of fruit can be poached in wine (pears in red wine is perhaps the best-known combination). If you find that you have a little faded (but not vinegary) Bordeaux or Burgundy, you could follow the example of cooks in both these regions by pouring the wine over fresh strawberries.

Riesling – As a general rule, Riesling can be used for almost any recipe that calls for white wine and grapes. It can also make a tasty difference to fresh fruit salad. Sweeter (Kabinett and Spätlese) Rieslings are widely used in Germany when cooking the veal and pork dishes that are so popular in that country, and chicken in a Riesling sauce is a delicious speciality of Alsace.

Sauternes – Like Champagne, Sauternes is often wrongly thought by cooks to be a catch-all term – in this case covering almost any kind of sweet white wine. In fact, however, the flavour you are looking for here is that of *botrytis*, the "noble rot" that gives almost any wine a peachy, dried-apricot flavour that, once tasted, is instantly recognizable.

Unfortunately, this is one area where you may find that you do have to spend a little extra on buying the right kind of wine because, unless it's a good example of Sauternes from a good vintage, it way well not have any of that flavour. You would do better to substitute a French alternative from Monbazillac, Loupiac or Ste-Croix-du-Mont or, more reliably, a German or Austrian Beerenauslese, an Alsatian Sélection de Grains Nobles or a "late-harvest" wine from Australia or California. Any such wine could be used to pour over peaches – or, inventively, to make a sauce Sauternes to serve with chicken, which gives it a wonderfully rich flavour.

Sherry – Some of the most unhelpful recipes of all are the ones that simply tell you to add sherry, without indicating what kind of sherry they mean, Sherry can be bone-dry, almost savoury – or Christmas-puddingy sweet. Bristol Cream will do your consommé no good at all, while the salty tang of manzanilla is not a flavour most people associate with sherry trifle. Swap the two styles and both dishes will be delicious. And bear in mind that dry sherry can be a handy substitute for the rice wine called for in Chinese recipes.

Wine in Restaurants

As recently as a decade ago, the cellars of better restaurants were piled high with well-chosen bottles of wine, laid down over the years so as to be precisely ready to drink on the evening when you or I ordered them from the list. Today, all that has changed; stocks of ready-to-drink old wine have evaporated under the heat of the accountants' and bankers' scrutiny. Some restaurateurs still cellar their wines, or buy at auction, but far too few bother – which explains why, traditional claret-drinkers who would ideally like to be drinking 20- and 25-year-old wines from the 1970s are offered examples which often have yet to celebrate their first decade. Fortunately, modern wine-making has given these bottles a youthful accessibility rarely found in the clarets of the past. Even so, paying a restaurant mark-up for a Bordeaux of the same age as the one in the local off-licence hardly adds to the magic of a special occasion.

Wine-waiters, too – in restaurants sufficiently ambitious to keep such a beast – are not always the fine and mature or dusty and aged specimens they once were. Many are young and enthusiastic; too many, however, persevere in trying to make the customer feel uncomfortable. This is, perhaps, a defensive measure against wine-literate diners, who have only to wander around the wine section of any good supermarket to know as much as – and maybe more than – their waiter about sparkling wines from the Penedés in Spain, Pinot Grigios from north-east Italy, the Rieslings of Washington State, Chardonnay from Australia's Hunter Valley, Cabernets from California and Sauvignons from New Zealand. Beware too, of sommeliers who helpfully seem to want you to spend rather more on a bottle than you intend. Very often, like car salesmen, they are paid a commission on sales, so while the waiter couldn't care less whether you have the oysters or the omelette, the sommelier may have a personal interest in persuading you of the merits of his priciest claret.

So, if you want to stay one step ahead of a sniffy or pushy sommelier, here's how to avoid the pitfalls of the restaurant wine list.

THE CHOICE

If your eye is immediately caught by wines of the kind listed on the left, you're off to a good start. A restaurateur with the confidence to choose and offer something a little different from the "standard" styles obviously takes an interest in what his customers are drinking, and may well

The sommelier should know every wine in his restaurant's cellar.

An attentive waiter will keep wine glasses topped up, but be wary of those who are overenthusiastic.

ensure that his staff are informed and ready to offer advice on unfamiliar wines. If you're still not quite confident about his powers of discrimination, order a glass of house red or white as an aperitif. If that's good, you can be pretty confident that somebody cares about the contents of the cellar; buying the kind of wine that is served by the glass calls for far more skill than listing a well known claret from a good vintage.

The Vintage

Any wine list that neglects to mention the vintages of the wines it lists clearly doesn't care about them or the drinker – but ones that print "1988/9" are no better. After all, they'd never dream of trying to sell you "Beef/Pork Casserole". Even when a vintage is named, beware of the switch 'twixt list and table. You order the 1990 and the stuff that is poured for you to taste is the 1992: be as firm as you would be if your avocado came with prawns when you ordered vinaigrette.

The Producer

Beware of lists that do not include the name of the producer alongside or beneath that of every wine. The omission does not necessarily mean that there will be no good wines on offer – just that their presence will be something of a fluke. And, like vintages, producers get switched too. You order the Sancerre produced by M. Dupont; the one with which you are presented is made by M. Chevalier, who might be a perfectly delightful man and a great trumpet-player in the village band – but a far worse wine-maker than his next-door neighbour Dupont.

Café life – small restaurant owners can often make good recommendations when it comes to their local wines.

THE PRICE

The price you pay for your meal and wine is up to the restaurateur and yourself; just remember, your readiness to hand over four times what he or she paid for an indifferent young Chablis merely helps to perpetuate a scandal. As a general rule, unless the restaurant is so luxurious that everything carries an in-built surcharge to cover the cost of the designer crockery, anything beyond two and a half times the retail price is completely out of court. A restaurateur's mark-up ought generally to be between 100 per cent and 200 per cent on the price he paid, which – to put this in perspective – is usually around 25 per cent less than the retail, by-the-bottle, price you would have to pay in most wine-merchants. While many restaurants add the same percentage mark-up to all their wines, some – more fairly – have a sliding scale which can make their classier bottles (on which they take a smaller margin) a better buy. Another reason for browsing at the top end of a good wine list is that it can yield unexpected bargains. The price of a mature Bordeaux, for example, may reflect the restaurant's profit on what was paid when the bottle was first bought a few years earlier. Some wines' prices have leapt so astronomically at auction however, that it is quite possible that restaurants are selling them more cheaply than you would find elsewhere.

THE SERVING

If you don't want to appear pretentious and silly, keep the sniffing and tasting ritual to a minimum. Some wine buffs seem to imagine that a protracted session of examining the

you like? If it's just a matter of the wine being too sweet or too dry for your taste, your right to send the wine back may be no greater than your right to complain that you don't like the tarragon in the sauce on the chicken. On the other hand, just as you would have every justification in returning a crème brulée served with cream that had gone sour, you have every reason to send back a wine that has something wrong with it. (For specific faults, see Tasting on p. 48.)

The Temperature

If your wine is too warm, ask for an ice bucket. Your wine-waiter will look down his nose when he realizes it's for the light red Loire or Beaujolais that he zealously parked in hot water in the kitchen for 10 minutes to bring it to the tepid state you find so unappealing, but don't be deterred – at least you will be able to drink and enjoy the wine in the way its maker intended. While it's chilling, sip slowly at a mean portion until the rest of the wine has cooled down – don't let the waiter hover over you carefully refilling your glass after every mouthful.

If the temperature of a white is too low, simply deter the waiter from replacing the bottle in the bucket. Let him top up your glass to his heart's content, cupping it meanwhile in your hands to warm the wine within.

cork, inhaling the wine and gargling with it are all some form of essential foreplay that mark the expert from the novice.

Not a bit of it. The real expert rarely pays much attention to the cork – provided that he or she has seen it being drawn from the bottle – but will usually satisfy him or herself with giving the wine the briefest of sniffs (just like the one you might give a carton of milk that's been in the fridge for a few days). If the wine smells fresh, clean and fruity, don't bother to taste it – just ask the waiter to serve.

The Taste

If you are not certain about the smell, take a sip. What if you then don't like it? Well, first things first. What don't

The Second Bottle

Half-way through the meal you absent-mindedly order another bottle of the Sancerre. What arrives could well be of a different vintage or by a different producer – or it could be a duff bottle of the same wine. So, make sure you get a look at the label and a taste of the wine before it's served – otherwise several half-full glasses of good wine from the first bottle could be spoiled by bad wine from the second.

The Tip

Very few wine-waiters get the chance to taste many of the wines they serve. If you have ordered one of the more interesting bottles from the list and the person who has served you has seemed enthusiastic and interested, invite him or her to taste it – or leave a little in the bottle.

Wine and Health

Nothing is quite clear in the alcohol-and-health debate, and matters are certainly not simplified when, on the one hand, dignified Frenchmen straightfacedly publish books suggesting that the wine from the village of Morgon in Beaujolais cures influenza while, on the other, anti-alcohol lobbyists refuse to discuss wine without bringing up references to motor accidents and the effects of violence committed by drunks.

Wine, like every other kind of alcohol, is of course a potentially dangerous substance – if it is abused and taken in excess. But this is no reason to treat it as a poison. After all, an overdose of nutmeg can be deadly, and no one has so far advocated posting health warnings on spice racks.

Besides, wine does have an extra-ordinarily honourable heritage in the annals of western civilization – as any book of quotations makes immediately clear. Excise it from the works of Chaucer, Shakespeare or Dickens – or the Bible for that matter – and you have to rewrite a large chunk of great literature. The "anti" lobby would argue that art and literature contain as many references to the damaging effects of drink. Where these occur, however, wine is rarely the culprit; what is more, the alcoholic drinks we consume today are very different to those of the past. The "gin" of Gin Lane was a rough, almost industrial spirit; Bill Sykes's violent outbursts were not the result of an excess of Muscadet.

CALORIES IN WINE BY STRENGTH AND SWEETNESS

This chart shows the variation in calorie content between different styles of wine – and whether the calories (kcal) come from the alcohol or the sugar. Figures are per 12.5 cl glass (approximately six measures per bottle) for table wines, and per 7 cl glass (16 measures per bottle) for fortified wines. 1 gm/litre sugar provides 3.75 kcal: 1 gm/litre alcohol (= 1% strength) provides 7 kcal.

TABLE WINE

	Strength	kcal	Sweetness	kcal	Total kcal
Low-alcohol	3.0%	26	40 gm/litre	2	28
Trocken (dry)	9.0%	79	0 gm/litre	0	79
Kabinett	9.0%	79	10 gm/litre	5	84
Moscato	6.5%	57.5	57 gm/litre	25.5	84
Vinho Verde	9.0%	79	10 gm/litre	5	84
Liebfraumilch	9.0%	79	15 gm/litre	7	86
Muscadet	11.5%	100	0 gm/litre	0	100
Claret	12.0%	105	0 gm/litre	0	105
Australian Chardonnay	13.0%	114	5 gm/litre	2	116
Châteauneuf-du-Pape/ Australian Red	14.0%	123	0 gm/litre	0	123

FORTIFIED WINE

	Strength	kcal	Sweetness	kcal	Total kcal
Dry sherry	17.0%	83	0 gm/litre	0	83
Sweet sherry	19.0%	94	130 gm/litre	34	127
Port	22.0%	108	100 gm/litre	27	135

Wine and Health

Sharing a glass of wine with a friend is a good way to unwind and can also be beneficial to one's health.

And, as a growing number of reports from around the world confirm, there is in any case now plenty of evidence that, far from being harmful, sensible levels of wine-drinking actually do contribute to good health.

First, there is the so-called French Paradox which became a catchphrase in America when it was revealed by CBS in its popular *60 Minutes* television programme that, despite their rich diet, wine-drinking Frenchmen had fewer heart attacks than health-conscious, non-drinking Americans. The research by French scientist Serge Renaud, which was the basis of that programme, was supported by a Danish study of 13,000 people, the results of which were published in 1995. Over 10 years, teetotallers had twice as much risk of dying as wine-drinkers with a daily intake of three to five glasses of wine. Reviewing these and other results, Dr Curt Ellison of Boston University was prepared to say that drinking one or two glasses of red wine with a daily meal will "most likely reduce the risk of heart disease". Taking the subject a little further, in 1995 Canadian writer Frank Jones published the *Save Your Heart Guide*, which provided credible scientific evidence for specifically recommending red Burgundy and other wines

Studies of drinking levels in France and other Mediterranean countries show that the number of heart attacks was far fewer than elsewhere.

made from the Pinot Noir grape as being especially effective against heart disease.

Other research has suggested that tannic red wine may even help to cure herpes, and prevent alzheimer's disease, while a study by the American Cancer Society, focusing on 250,000 subjects, suggested that a drink a day (though not necessarily of wine) reduced their chances of getting cancer by 10 per cent.

On the other hand, much work remains to be done on wine and allergies. Some people seem to develop an intolerance to red or white wine - and even particular types of wine - which causes them to suffer headaches or to come out in a rash.

WINE AND OTHER KINDS OF ALCOHOL

There have been various research projects devoted to the question of whether wine is a healthier form of alcohol than beer or spirits. Though none has reached a satisfactory conclusion, most suggest that wine in general, and red wine in particular, does seem to have the edge over other drinks.

WINE STRENGTH

Wines can vary in strength from the non-alcohol and low-alcohol styles, which range from zero to 5 per cent, to fortified wines that can weigh in at as much as 27 per cent (nearly three-quarters the strength of whisky, and usually served in rather larger measures). In general, however, most table wines and fizz have strengths of between 9 per cent and 13 per cent, and most fortified wines – such as sherry or port – average 15–20 per cent.

To help people to drink sensibly, the system of "units" used in the table on page 75 illustrates how strengths can vary. A 12.5 cl glass of German wine at 8 per cent is most convenient, containing just one unit of alcohol. But if you fancy a change – a big Châteauneuf, for example – that figure could virtually double.

It is generally considered that the maximum advisable number of units of alcohol for any man to consume in a week is 21–35. For women the figure is lower – 14–21 – which may seem unfair, but in fact there is a wealth of evidence to prove that, because of their lower body mass but relatively higher proportion of body fat, women metabolize alcohol less efficiently than men. Some doctors

also recommend an alcohol-free day or two per week, while the Danish study contradictorily suggests that the most beneficial effects are felt if the wine is taken in moderate daily doses rather than weekend binges.

WINE AND WEIGHT

Wine is fattening – like almost everything else we enjoy eating and drinking. Alcohol is actually more fattening than sugar; drinking a strong dry white wine like a 14 per cent Meursault will put more weight on you than than a hock which is sweeter but has less alcohol – or a light-bodied red, such as a 12.5 per cent claret. However, there is some evidence that the way wine aids digestion of food, may slightly mitigate its own calorific effect.

WINE AND PREGNANCY

Less than 50 years after doctors routinely recommended mothers-to-be to build themselves up with Guinness, barmen in the US now treat pregnant customers like prospective murderers. Today, women are not only officially told to lay off alcohol while expecting but, according to some research, would be wise to stick to soft drinks prior to conception – though if too many took this advice a great deal of conception would probably never occur in the first place! Curiously, in European wine-producing countries, where the Foetal Alcohol Syndrome which so worries North Americans is almost unknown, pregnant women often do continue drinking before, during and after pregnancy – but in far greater moderation.

WINE AND DRIVING

Sorry, but if you want to drive safely – never mind legally – there are no get-out clauses or loopholes. Tests have proved that while it tends to promote feelings of confidence, even the smallest amount of alcohol in the bloodstream can impair judgement – especially in people who are tired or in any other way under the weather. To be safe at the wheel, the only answer is to drink no wine at all – or, for those extraordinarily self-conscious individuals who claim to "feel silly" holding an orange juice, one that has been de-alcoholized.

WINE AND FOOD

To most southern Europeans, food and wine are two halves of a whole; they rarely consume one without the other. Just as their lunch or dinner almost always includes wine, the glass of red they order in a pavement café is usually accompanied by savoury titbits. It's a habit worth adopting; and it may help the wine perform the medical miracles described above.

WINE AND TIME

The average human body takes around an hour to deal with a single glass of average-strength wine. Heavily built men may find that they can cope with more than this; lighter men and most women, however, may equally discover this to be too rapid a rate of input for their bodies.

Although it is advisable to accompany any alcohol with food, and to punctuate it with the occasional glass of water or other non-alcoholic drink (to counteract the alcohol's dehydrating effects), it has to be said that there is no effective way to speed up the process of metabolizing the alcohol. The supposed capacity of black coffee to achieve this is a myth. Similarly, excessive drinking with dinner can leave you with alcohol in your bloodstream the following morning.

HANGOVERS

Even the most sensible drinkers sometimes suffer the consequences of swallowing too much of a good thing – especially if they forget to down a pint or so of water (more if possible) to ward off the effects of alcohol-induced dehydration.

If it's too late for prevention, is there a cure? Ignore any advice to indulge in the hair of any species of dog – that's an anaesthetic, not a remedy – and stick to easily digestible protein, and plenty of liquids such as orange or tomato juice with which to rehydrate the body. Vitamin B tablets are another lifesaver on the morning after the night before, partly because alcohol reduces the ability of the body to assimilate the vitamin. Evening Primrose Oil also seems to help on the morning after the night before.

As a final hint, beware particularly of over-indulging in vintage port, whose reputation as hangover-fare is wholly earned. Tawny will leave you feeling fitter.

Organic Wine

Until man learned how to manufacture chemical herbicides, fungicides, insecticides and fertilizers, grape-growing and wine-making were tricky, unpredictable tasks, at the annual mercy of all manner of hazards. On the other hand, there was one way in which life in the vineyard was actually better then: everything was in some kind of balance.

Today, even some of the most vociferous of "non-organic" grape growers would agree that the growing immunity of the pests and the deficiencies in the overworked, over-treated soil are creating a vicious circle in which scientists are driven to develop ever more sophisticated treatments.

"Organic" producers want to break that cycle by giving nature more of a chance to manage its own affairs, allowing "good" bugs to kill "bad" ones and encouraging the natural organisms – up to a billion per gram – within the soil to recreate its essential balance. Some of these vinous reactionaries – or should we call them revolutionaries? – follow "biodynamic" practices which can seem downright eccentric, including sprinkling the earth with herbs on days chosen according to the phases of the moon. But before you mock these activities, pull the cork on a bottle from the Domaine Leroy in Burgundy or from Didier Dagueneau, or Nicolas Joly's Roche aux Moines vineyard in the Loire – and think again. These wines, made in some of the most climatically hazardous vineyards in the world, are leagues ahead of the stuff made by their more conventional neighbours.

Organic viticulture, like the political movement it often resembles, comes in many different flavours. While those small producers are out scattering powdered quartz and infusions of nettles and camomile on their vines, huge companies like Fetzer and Mondavi in California and Penfolds and BRL Hardy in Australia are now making large quantities of organic wine. It is no accident that these bigger producers are all in the New World, where climatic conditions are relatively predictable. But with firms like these already on board, the organic bandwagon is sure to attract more passengers.

Beware though of wine-makers whose organic credentials can sometimes prove to be very questionable – and pay equal heed to producers who quietly suggest that,

Some organic vineyards grow fruit and vegetables as well.

Cover crops, like clover, grown below vines provide nutrients.

Composted pumice is an acceptable form of fertilizer for organic vineyards.

without making a fuss about it, they might be making wines that were more authentically organic than the ones on offer from some of their supposedly "green"-fingered competitors.

ORGANIC WINE-MAKING: HOW IT DIFFERS

In theory, it is quite possible to produce wine simply by crushing grapes, allowing them to ferment and bottling the resulting liquid. Unfortunately, as most home wine-makers will have discovered, wines made in this way often stop tasting good within a very, very short time.

Vines and grapes are subject to all kinds of pests, fungi and diseases that can either prevent growers from making any wine at all, or leave them with a drink that has the unpleasant musty smell and taste of rotten grapes. Once it has been made, wine is similarly subject to the attentions of various kinds of bacteria that are eager to convert it into vinegar.

In the vineyard, there are a number of chemical sprays that can be used to protect the vines from rot and insects; in the winery, producers almost always have to use sulphur dioxide as an antiseptic to ward off bacterial infection. In addition, wine-growers can, for example, use fertilizers to increase the yields of their vines.

Organic Wine

When fining their wine, European wine-makers can (though rarely, and only under supervision) legally use potassium ferrocyanide instead of such traditional agents as powdered clay, milk protein, beaten egg white, fish scales or even ox blood. In principle, the fining agent does not combine with the wine, merely passing through it – dragging, as it sinks, any solid matter with it – but very few conscientious producers, organic or otherwise, believe this sufficiently to use potassium ferrocyanide. Indeed, the substance is banned from use in this way in the USA.

Organic wine-makers aim to avoid all unnecessary use of chemicals and accept the lower yields of non-fertilized vines. (In warm, dry climates, this involves rather fewer sacrifices than in the cooler, wetter regions of northern Europe, where growers who do not spray their vines can sometimes lose an entire crop.) In the winery, organic producers use as little sulphur dioxide as possible, and fine with natural materials such as egg white.

So far, so good – and very laudable too. Unfortunately, the problem for anyone who would rather drink wine made by these producers is that it is often difficult to know how to differentiate it from other, less "organic" wines. Some labels carry the symbols of various associations – but some top-class organic wine-makers neglect to pin their colours to the mast.

The avowedly organic wine-makers form an incredibly loose-knit band of separate associations around the world, each of which has its own insignia and rules and – in some cases – petty jealousies. To compound the confusion, at least one such organic association in France is actually funded by the manufacturers of organic products for use by the growers: use our products, and you're a member of the club.

CRIME AND PUNISHMENT

In 1984, the news broke that samples of Austrian wine had been found to contain substantial doses of DEG – diethylene glycol – a chemical most easily described as first cousin to anti-freeze, and harmful if drunk in large quantities. As laboratories in several countries analysed thousands of samples of wine, it was discovered that wines from Germany and Italy contained the chemical too – though in far smaller proportions.

Despite initial claims that DEG was just another of the naturally occurring chemicals found in all food and drink, it rapidly became apparent that the only way that the chemical could have got into the wine was for someone to have put it there – to "enrich" its flavour. The reason the German and Italian wines contained such small amounts was that their producers had almost certainly not added it to their vats themselves, but had beefed up their wine with bought-in wine or grape concentrate which had – unknown to them – been adulterated.

What became known as the "Anti-Freeze Scandal" was followed by a far more serious – indeed fatal – case of fakery in Italy, in which, it was said, only Italian bureaucracy saved those responsible for adding a dangerous industrial alcohol to wine from standing trial for manslaughter.

The Austrian and Italian scandals of the 1980s have made the authorities throughout the world so sensitive to how wine ought and ought not to be made that, in 1990, a number of Chilean wines were removed from the shelves in Britain because they had been found to contain sorbitol, a harmless and natural ingredient that is legitimately added in the making of all sorts of foods and drinks, yet is illegal in wine.

The wine-drinkers of the past were far less well protected, for wine has been faked and adulterated in one way or another for almost as long as it has been drunk. Virgil, predicting that "The ripening grape shall hang on every thorn", had no doubt that crooks in cold countries where vines could not be grown would pass off as "wine" the fermented juice of whatever fruit they found in the hedgerow.

In the nineteenth century, the French author Stendhal recorded visiting a factory in France where, "Out of wine, sugar, iron filings, and some flower essences they make the wines of every country." Far more often, though, wine merchants merely blended in wines from other regions. Pale burgundy would be enriched with a dollop of thick, dark wine from North Africa; claret was quite openly "improved" by the addition of a little wine from Hermitage, on the other side of France.

In the 1970s, Bordeaux was rocked by the revelation that Cruse, one of the city's best-known and most respected merchants, was selling fake wines and illegal blends under the names of popular appellations. That scandal led to a tightening-up of the regulations in France and elsewhere in Europe, but wine crime has proved as impossible to eradicate as any other. In the 1980s, batches of false Moët et Chandon found in the USA were traced back to South Africa, while an Italian gang was found to have created false bottles of Mumm Champagne. It was only by chance, in late 1994, that the highly regarded Domaine de Malandes in Chablis discovered that crooks in Germany were using a forgery of its labels to sell a blend of cheap *vin de pays* and German wine as Grand Cru Chablis. If the Saarbrucken discount store in which the wine was on offer had not advertised it at a ludicrously low price, no one might have noticed until the fake wine had all been sold. The best insurance for a consumer against this kind of fraud is to buy your wine from a company that cares about the quality and authenticity of what it is selling.

Learning about Wine

Wine, like gardening, cooking and, now I come to think of it, sex, is one of those subjects that you really can't learn all about from books. As a writer, I can describe all sorts of smells and flavours and their relationship to all sorts of wines. But nothing can compete with the experience of sniffing and tasting a wine for yourself – and of comparing the impact different and similar wines have on your nose and tongue.

So, apart from reading a book such as this, I'm afraid you're going to have to do some practical study with bottles, glasses and a corkscrew. One way to do this is to sign up for evening wine classes. There are various examples of these on offer in most major cities and, like classes in every other subject, their quality depends on the teacher, the course materials and the other students. Courses run by organisations such as the British Wine & Spirits Education Trust, Christies and Sothebys and major universities can be relied upon to give you good quality intruction. Other quite pricy courses can be quite disappointing so, before parting with any serious money, I'd recommend that you ask precisely which wines you will be tasting and the background of the lecturer.

Similarly, when signing up for a food-and-wine course, it is worth checking to make sure that the wine element has not simply been half-heartedly tacked onto the cookery classes.

If studying wine in your home town is fun, it hardly compares to the experience of visiting a wine region and doing your studies on the spot. The same warnings about the quality of the teaching naturally apply to wine tours and classes – but if travelling overseas, you may also need to make sure that there aren't going to be any language barriers between the you and the wine and the teaching.

The simplest, and in some ways, arguably the best way to build up your knowledge and confidence is to get together with a few friends, and a few bottles that have been wrapped in aluminium foil or brown paper to conceal their identities. Knowledge brings prejudice. If you know that a wine is an expensive Bordeaux or a cheap offering from Bulgaria you are almost certain to have an idea of the quality and style you are likely to expect. So be ready to taste the wines "blind" and to give your honest opinion of how it strikes you and what you think it is. Of course, you will make a fool of yourself by wrongly identifying all sorts of bottles, but don't worry, so almost certainly will your friends and fellow tasters. Besides, even the world's most famous experts regularly fall flat on their tasting faces – indeed it was one such highly respected expert, Harry Waugh who, when asked if he had ever mistaken a Bordeaux for a Burgundy, memorably replied, "Not since lunch." Remember, learning about wine is just like learning about anything else: you will gain more from the mistakes you make than from the things you get right. The more you practice, the more likely you are to score the wine equivalent of the hole-in-one: the precisely correct identification of a wine's origin and vintage.

While the range of wines on the market today is so huge that it is tempting to try to learn about every style and nationality at once, I'd recommend that you try to focus as much of your attention on a type of wine that you really enjoy. Gaining an in-depth knowledge of, say, red Burgundy or Californian Zinfandel, is like learning to play a particular instrument. Once you can pick out a tune confidently on the piano, it is not too difficult to switch to the guitar. And much the same can be said of wine.

The good thing about a wine course is that it involves lots of practical work!

THE WINE QUALIFICATIONS

Every country has its own wine qualifications. Some places, such as the USA, France and Japan particularly favour the wine courses that have been devised for people who are going to serve wine in restaurants. In each of these countries, a qualified sommelier is among the most respected members of the industry and a wine waiter who has won a regional, national or international *"Meilleur Sommelier"* competition will be treated like a sports champion. Britain, for some reason takes its sommeliers less seriously but, as the traditional trading centre of the wine world, it has instead devised its own set of qualifications including the Master of Wine certificate which is globally recognised as the toughest set of written and tasting exams of all.

Most years, fewer than a dozen applicants pass, and fewer than 250 people have been awarded the qualification.

What to Buy

This is the fun part – deciding what you're going to put into your cellar, and how much you're going to spend. I've given suggestions for some well balanced selections here, but you'll have your own tastes and needs to accommodate. Any good wine merchant should be pleased to advise you if you want to splash out on a "ready-made" cellar – or you may want to build up your selection slowly. With suitable storage space to hand, you'll be able to stock up on good buys as and when you come across them – and store up a great deal of future drinking pleasure.

It may seem obvious, but if you're buying wine to drink, then stick to what you like. In other words, if your passion is Burgundy, then don't be pressurized into buying lots of Bordeaux just because everybody says it's a must-have vintage. If you never eat fish, then you won't need so much white; if port gives you a headache, then it's not a bargain, no matter how low the price.

A good wine shop will often invite customers to taste its wares.

What to Buy

Some things are hard to miss! Wine merchants will go to any lengths to advertise!

WHERE TO BUY?

Until the middle of the twentieth century, there were only three ways to buy wine: directly from the producer's cellar, at auction or from a merchant who would almost certainly have been an independent business offering the same kind of personal attention as a tailor. In those days, the merchant would deal personally with his (wine was a male preserve) customers whom he probably inherited from their fathers and grandfathers. Then the supermarkets and the retail chains arrived and the picture changed completely. Of course traditional merchants still exist – thank goodness –and there are regions, such as New York State for example, where supermarkets are forbidden to sell alcohol, but most of us now do most of our wine shopping in self-service outlets where service is, at best, cursory.

Some of these big retailers – in the UK in particular – take trouble over the quality of the wines they sell; others – in the United States and France respectively – are often happy to stock a wide range of widely advertised brands and well-known appellations irrespective of the way they taste. When buying from a big retailer, your choice of purchase will more than likely be dictated by price, previous experience, recommendation (from a friend or the media) or by the "shelf-talkers" and other forms of promotion in the shop. A word of warning here. In wine, as anything else,

What to Buy

BEST CELLARS

It is as impossible to recommend an ideal cellar for a complete stranger as it is to advise them on the ideal contents of their wardrobe. However, this is my personal selection.

Bordeaux – Médoc: Châteaux Léoville Lascases, Palmer, Léoville-Barton, Pichon-Longueville-Lalande, Pichon-Longueville, Lynch-Bages, Ducru-Beaucaillou, Cos d'Estournel, Palmer, La Gurgue, Haut-Bages-Libéral, Chasse-Spleen; Graves: Domaine de Chevalier, Châteaux la Louvière, Fieuzal, Haut-Bailly (red); Pomerol and St Emilion, and satellites: Châteaux Pavie, Figeac, Lafleur, Le Bon Pasteur, Certan-de-May, Vieux-Château-Certan, Haut Bertinerie, Puygeraud, Canon (Canon-Fronsac); Sauternes and Barsac: Châteaux Rieussec, Gilette, Bastor-Lamontagne, Doisy-Daëne.

Burgundy – Nuits St Georges: Gouges, A Michelot, Faiveley; Vosne Romanée: D Rion, Méo-Camuzet; Volnay: M Lafarge, Pousse d'Or; Meursault: Michelot-Buisson, Lafon; Puligny-Montrachet: Carillon, Leflaive, Chartron et Trébuchet, Verget; Chassagne-Montrachet: Carillon, Sauzet.

Rhône – Hermitage: Chave, Guigal; Crozes-Hermitage: Graillot; Côte Rôtie: Guigal, Jaboulet Ainé; Châteauneuf-du-Pape: Château Beaucastel.

Southern France – Mas de Daumas Gassac, Domaine de Trevallon, Domaine Hortus, Château Vignelaure.

Barolo – Elio Altare, G Mascarello, Aldo Conterno.

Italian superstars – Gaja, Sassicaia, Tignanello, Solaia, Cepparello.

Rioja – Campillo, Contino, Remelluri Martinez Bujanda, Marques de Riscal.

Navarra – Chivite.

Spanish superstars – Pesquera, Vega Sicilia, Jean Leon Cabernet, Marques de Griñon, Torres Mas la Plana and Milmanda Chardonnay.

Germany – Mosel: Dr Loosen, Egon Müller, Deinhard, F W Gymnasium; Rhine/Nahe: Balthasar Ress, Burklin-Wolf, Bassermann-Jordan, Müller Cattoir, Tony Jost, Kurt Darting.

Champagne – Pol Roger, Dom Ruinart, Charles Heidsieck, Bollinger, Roederer, Salon, Billecart-Salmon, Gosset, Deutz, Krug. Vintage and tawny port Dow's, Graham's, Taylor's, Niepoort, Fonseca-Guimaraens, Noval, Quinta de la Rosa, Quinta do Crasto. Top-quality sherry Barbadillo, Gonzalez Byass, Lustau.

Other sparkling wine – "J" by Jordan, J Schram, Scharffenberger, Croser, Iron Horse, Green Point from Chandon, Roederer Estate (Quartet).

Cabernet Sauvignon – Penfolds Bin 707 (Aus.), Coleraine (NZ), Mondavi Reserve (Cal.), Laurel Glen.

Chardonnay – Kumeu River (NZ), Leeuwin Estate, Petaluma (Aus.), Inniskillin (Canada), Hargrave (Long Island), Sonoma Cutrer, Simi, Kistler (Cal.).

Sauvignon Blanc – Cloudy Bay (NZ), Cullens (Aus.), Thelema (SA), Casablanca Vineyards (Chile).

Sémillon – McWilliams, Tyrrells (Aus.).

Riesling – Hardy's Siegersdorf, Grosset, Petaluma, Knappstein (Aus.), Renaissance (Cal.).

Pinot Noir – Martinborough, Fromm (NZ), Dom Drouhin (Oregon), Hamilton Russell (SA), Saintsbury, Au Bon Climat (Cal.), Coldstream Hills, Wignalls, Bass Philip (Aus.).

Merlot – Matanzas Creek, Newton (Cal.), Casa Lapostolle (Chile).

Syrah/Shiraz – Penfolds Grange etc, Yalumba, Hardy's, Yarra Yering, Henschke, Peter Lehman (Aus.), Phelps, Bonny Doon (Cal.).

Zinfandel – Ridge, Ravenswood (Cal.), Cape Mentelle (Aus.). Late-harvest and fortified, Petaluma, Brown Bros Orange Muscat and Flora, Morris Liqueur Muscat (Aus.), Phelps, Renaissance (Cal.).

Supermarkets and hypermarkets are offering a wider and wider choice to customers.

there are plenty of bargains to be had, but not nearly as many as there appear to be. That cheap bottle of Château X may prove to be less of a good buy when you realise that it was made in the duff 1997 vintage rather than the more desirable 1996. The same applies to trusting your memory of recommendations. Unless you have got precise details of the producer or brand and the *cuvée*, grape variety or vineyard and vintage, there's a strong risk of getting a less good bottle than you expect. The store's shelf-talkers – often including quotes and marks out of 100 or competition medals – can be useful, but bear in mind that these, like the adjectives on movie posters, by definition offer a partial view. One critic may have liked the wine; others might have hated it. So check to be sure that the critic or competition is one in which you have confidence.

Serious stuff! Tasting wine prior to an auction.

GOING TO THE SOURCE

Of course the one person who is least likely to offer you an unbiased opinion about a wine is the man or woman who produced it, but there are plenty of compensations in dealing with them directly. Indeed, filling your cellar from the one in which the wine was made can be the most enjoyable way of all, and there is little to beat the experience of seeing the vines, presses, tanks and barrels that were involved in its production. Throughout the wine-making world, producers of every size – from one-man-band operations to giants like Moët & Chandon and Robert Mondavi – happily welcome visitors and prospective customers. In some cases you'll be received personally by the wine-maker or a member of his or her family; in others there might be a more or less well informed guide, or quite possibly a person with a cash register who barely knows how to handle a corkscrew. If you are lucky enough to find a person who does know what they are talking about, take advantage of the chance to ask questions. How long should you keep the wine before opening it? What temperature should it be served at? Is it

What to Buy

worth decanting? What dishes does it go with best? What is the difference between one vintage and another? What do these words mean on the label? Which other producers in the region might be worth visiting?

So much for the information; now it's time to do some shopping. My first rule is that unless you already know the producer's wines, don't be persuaded to buy without tasting. On the other hand, don't go into a cellar expecting anyone to open a large number of bottles just for you. Remember, once its cork has been pulled, the wine can't be sold to anyone else. When visiting smaller producers, bear in mind too that the time they are spending with you on a weekend afternoon, might otherwise be devoted to their vines or wines – or their families. So, as a car dealer might say, if you're not a genuine buyer, don't hang around kicking the tyres.

SEEING A SPECIALIST

Buying from a specialist wine merchant either in the flesh or by mail or over the phone has – or should have – the advantage of coming with pre- and after-sales service. A good merchant will often have dealt with the producer directly, so he or she should know all about the wines he or she is selling: when they should be drunk and with which kind of dish. There may also be tastings at which you can sample ranges of wines, newsletters and a website to keep you informed of new arrivals and special offers. In some instances you may have to purchase your bottles by the dozen – but they will not necessarily have to be full of the same wine. Perhaps the most appealing aspect, though, is the mutually beneficial relationship that can be struck up with a merchant: you tell him or her how you liked wines you have bought, and they use this information to recommend bottles you are likely to enjoy.

WINE AND AUCTIONS

Until ebay.com, amazon.com, winebid.com, Sotheby's and their ilk all introduced us to the notion of bidding for wine over the internet, competing with others to buy bottles at auction was generally thought of as the preserve of pin-striped British merchants and ludicrously wealthy "collectors" seeking to add to the thousand or so priceless clarets already in their cellar. But wine auctions are – and have always been – a great way for anyone to buy all sorts of wines, including some pretty humble daily-drinking fare. While many of the lots are submitted by wine traders and collectors, there are also wines from bankrupt restaurants and the private cellars unhappily disposed of under pressure from divorce lawyers.

You won't often have the chance to taste before buying under the hammer, so tread carefully. The auctioneer's catalogue should provide invaluable background information about where and how the wine has been stored. A good auction house will try to ensure that it hasn't

been spoiled by being stacked next to a central heating boiler, but some auctioneers are less careful. Contents of big private cellars are likely to have been properly looked after – as will wine sold at auction by merchants. Take note of the fact that the wine you want to buy might need to be transported – at your expense – from its current owner's cellar – or a bonded warehouse which will require you to pay duty before releasing it. Costs like these have to be added to the bidding price, as will a "buyer's premium" and quite possibly some form of Value Added or other sales tax.

Work out what all these costs might represent before you begin to raise your hand – otherwise, you might end up paying more for your bottles than you'd hand over the counter at your local shop. But don't let these warnings deter you from the idea of buying at auction. There is a peculiar hunter-like pleasure in serving and drinking a wine you had to wrest frrom another eager bidder.

WINE AND THE NET

As the twentieth century drew to a close, the way we all buy wine – and just about everything else – began to undergo an extraordinary metamorphosis. Instead of walking into a shop or perusing a catalogue, suddenly, a growing number of us discovered that we could use a mouse and a screen to make our purchases online

Now that we are beginning to take buying over the Net for granted, it is worth looking back at the way wine first featured on what used to be called the world wide web. Before what similarly used to be called the information superhighway was covered in tarmac and lined by advertising hoardings and stores, a small number of wine enthusiasts discovered that the internet provided an ideal means of communication with each other. Compuserve and America Online and hundreds of so-called .alt groups offered forums in which Marvin in Los Angeles could

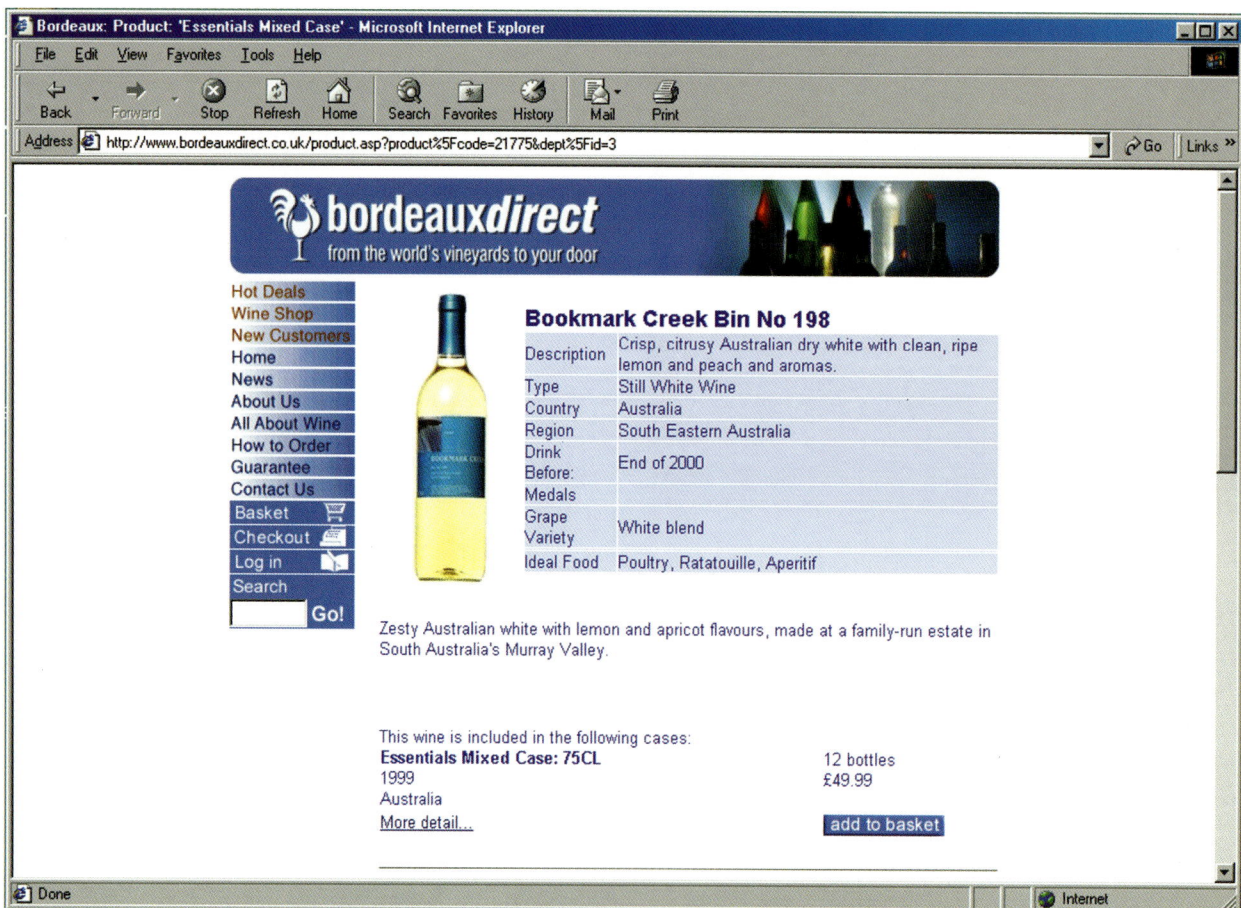

Above and opposite: many companies now have websites offering a host of information on wines as well as ordering facilities.

What to Buy

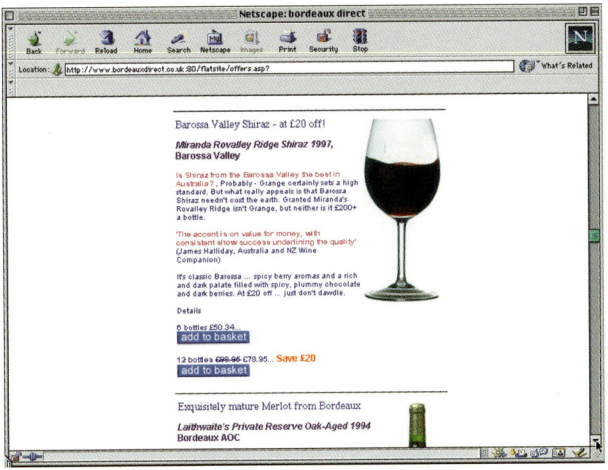

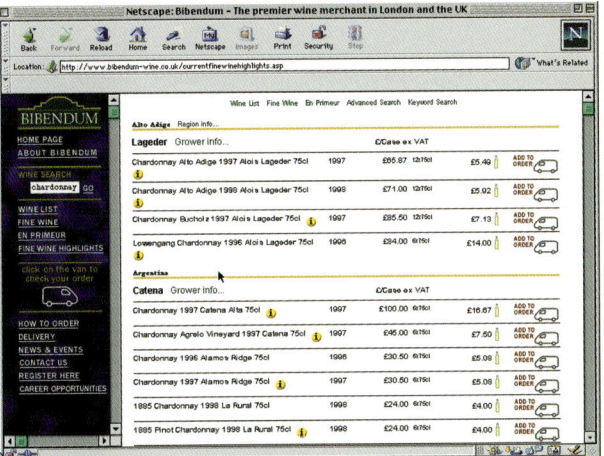

exchange views on the flavour of his 1986 Château Beychevelle with Matthew in London and Michel in Lyon. Discussion boards on which messages could be left and responded to were followed by chat rooms where the discussion was live – if not always lively.

Like the rest of the Internet at the time, most of this activity was frankly, not to say proudly, non-commercial. Then, as a few more enterprising producers such as Château Haut-Brion and Robert Mondavi created sites to tell people all about where they were and what they were doing, a growing number of entrepreneurial retailers realised that wine, like books and CDs was an ideal product to sell online. Sites like Virtual Vineyards – now wine.com – were among the first to set up their stalls, but others such as the 250-year-old Berry Brothers & Rudd in London soon joined them, along with online auctioneers and magazines. By early 2001, dozens of newly-launched "dot-com" companies were all rushing to claim their slice of the market.

Ironically, given all this activity, wine is still handicapped in comparison with most of the other products and services we buy online. In simple terms, wine is one of the few things whose trade is infuriatingly restricted by local and national governments. So, there are numerous States of the Union whose residents are legally prevented from buying from other parts of their own nation, and British wine drinkers – unlike most of their fellow Europeans – cannot simply order wine to be delivered directly from a producer in France, Italy or Spain; they have to go to collect it themselves.

Delivery of wine is made no easier by the nature of the beast. Bottles are not easy to transport. They are heavy – around a kilo apiece – and doubly fragile: if you drop them they break, and if you let them get too hot or cold they spoil. The person to whom the wine is to be delivered needs to be there to receive his or her wine when it arrives. Leaving a delivery of top class Cabernet Sauvignon outside a house on a sunny day in Arizona is a rather worse idea than leaving a few books or CDs.

As with any other aspect of the Internet, the picture is changing and evolving so quickly that it is unwise, not to say impossible, to predict how the relationship between wine and the Internet will develop. It is, however, already clear that there are a number of things that the Net will do consumately well. First, there its established role as a means of communication between wine lovers. The only difference is that the growing ease of communication will mean that instead of laboriously typing out "v e r y t a n n i c" on your keyboard, you will be sipping and speaking to a camera while watching your fellow enthusiasts doing the same on your TV screen. There is no reason today why 10, 100, or 1,000 people around the world could not simultaneously taste a new vintage and share their reactions. This democratisation may help to undermine the often overweaning influence of US critics like Robert Parker and the *Wine Spectator*. After all, if the marketing of a low-budget film like the *Blair Witch Project* could sidestep the critics, why couldn't a wine producer pull off the same trick?

The net can also provide a wealth of education and information (through sites like winepros.com, wine-school.com and food-and-wine.com with which I am involved and through a plethora of sites hosted by regions, producers and merchants) that is currently unavailable elsewhere. In the future, the Internet might prove almost as invaluable to wine drinkers as a corkscrew.

Facts and Fallacies

There are all kinds of misconceptions about wine – many of them wilfully promoted by the people who make the stuff, and by lazy wine-writers who merely copy what they have read elsewhere. Which is why I thought it might he a good idea to dispel some of these illusions. And to reveal a few hard-to-believe facts about wine that are guaranteed to be authentic.

Sherry lasts indefinitely
The sweeter styles will keep but, even before you pull the cork, dry fino and manzanilla sherries may have lost their original, tangy freshness. So avoid leaving the bottle hanging around before you open it – and drink it up within the week. If you are likely to take longer than that, either pour half the sherry into a half-bottle when you first open it – or, wiser still, buy it in a half-bottle in the first place.

Sherry, port and Champagne can be made anywhere
In the USA, though not in Oregon where stricter rules apply, all sorts of cheap fizzy wine can call itself Champagne. In Europe, however, reasonable EC regulations forbid the sale of "Champagne" made anywhere outside the French region of that name. Likewise, genuine sherry only comes from Spain and port from the Douro in Portugal.

Canadian, Japanese and British wine is made from grapes grown respectively in Canada, Japan and Britain
Canada and Japan traditionally make wine from their own grapes but also import grape concentrate from South America and bottle it as local produce (Ontario and British Columbia both grow wine grapes but "Quebec wine" will almost certainly come from a long way further south).

"British" wine – unlike English wine (which confusingly includes Welsh wine) is actually produced by a British technique of diluting and fermenting the grape concentrate which, in this instance, tends to come from Cyprus.

In fact, under European law, none of these reconstituted drinks is defined as "wine" which, by the EC definition, has to be made from freshly picked grapes. English wine is the real stuff – though even this is allowed to contain a little sweetening juice from Germany.

Red Bordeaux is made from the Cabernet Sauvignon
Well, quite a lot of it is – but actually, the Merlot is the most widely planted grape in Bordeaux. And in the communes of St Emilion and Pomerol, the blend is often just Merlot and Cabernet Franc.

All wines improve with age
This is a belief still common in the countries of southern and eastern Europe and South America, where older wines are thought to be better by definition and people have become used to drinking wine with the taste of oxidation – the sherry-like character of wines that are past their best. Most modern wine-drinkers now prefer wines with fresher, fruitier flavours. Almost all inexpensive white wines should be drunk within a couple of years (at most) of the harvest, and even Bordeaux may need drinking young in vintage.

Cheap wines don't travel
Some don't – but then again, nor do some frail, old, expensive ones. In the case of young, cheap wine, everything depends on the way it has been produced. Well-made wine, whatever its price, should have no difficulty in being carried from one side of the world to the other. When a wine you enjoyed on holiday and brought back with you doesn't taste quite the same at home, it's very likely to be because the circumstances have changed, not the wine.

Facts and Fallacies

INCREDIBLE – BUT TRUE

According to the *Guinness Book of Records*, the longest distance a cork has flown from an untreated, unheated Champagne bottle is 54.18 metres. The previous record was beaten at Woodbury Winery and Cellars, in New York state, on June 5 1988, by Professor Emeritus Heinrich Medicus.

The tallest Champagne fountain was built – where else? – in Las Vegas at Caesar's Palace, required 23,642 traditional long-stemmed glasses and rose 47 glass storeys – 7.85 m/25 ft 9 in. And the Champagne? That was Moët & Chandon.

The highest price ever paid for a wine at auction was the £105,000 paid at Christie's in London for a 1787 "Jefferson" Château Lafite whose bottle was engraved with the US President's initials and is supposed to have been bought by him while he was serving as a diplomat in France. In November 1986, 11 months after the sale, the cork, dried out by the exhibition lights, slipped into the bottle, allowing its contents to become, in their turn, the world's most expensive bottle of old vinegar.

A similarly impressive sum – Fr8,600 – was paid for another Guinness record-holder, a glass of 1993 Beaujolais Nouveau which was auctioned for charity in the cellar of Pickwick's pub in Beaune within hours of its first release to the market.

A wine whose label declares its vintage to be 1985 could have been made from grapes which were picked in 1986. "Eiswein" is a German and Austrian style made from grapes that have been left to freeze on the vine. Sometimes, the wine-growers have to wait so long for the necessary severe frost that they do not harvest the grapes until January, three or four months after the grapes for more conventional wines have been picked.

A teaspoon suspended in an opened bottle of Champagne will help it to keep its fizz. Even the experts at Moët & Chandon admit that they are foxed as to why this works – but it does.

Mikhail Gorbachev was an enemy of wine who introduced a scheme to uproot vineyards in several regions of the former Soviet Union, as part of a campaign to combat the alcoholism that costs tens of thousands of lives per year. During the heyday of the Communist regime, however, wine was shipped from one republic to another, sometimes swapped litre-for-litre for petrol.

In the US, the label of every wine sold has to be approved by the authorities – which explains why, on occasion, wines from such illustrious producers as Château Mouton Rothschild have been outlawed because their labels were thought to be too sexy.

Spain has the largest area of vineyards in the world – but ranks only third in terms of production; low rainfall makes for low yields per vine. Similarly, Spain's Airén, one of the most unmemorable grape varieties, is still the most widely planted, though again production is, thank goodness, relatively small.

The international success of Australia's wines in the 1980s and 1990s was so great that exports rose in the decade or so up to 1994 from around 10 million bottles to nearly 150 million.

China and Taiwan increased their vineyards from 34,000 ha (84,000 acres) in the early 1980s to 168,000 ha (415,000 acres) in 1993. With an annual production of around 500 million bottles, they now account for over 1 per cent of the world's wine harvest.

One American wine company – E & J Gallo – produces more wine each year than the whole of Champagne.

White grapes have to be used in red Chianti. Not because they improve its flavour, but because this bit of Tuscany has a surplus of white grapevines. The obligatory dose in Chianti Classico is so small, however, at 2–5 per cent, that the law cannot be enforced. Wine-growers in Hermitage in the Rhône and in Rioja in Spain, however, can voluntarily choose to put some white grapes in their red wine.

A copper coin can remove a nasty smell from a wine. If the wine smells like rotten eggs, the chances are that some of the sulphur dioxide used in its preparation has turned into hydrogen sulphide. Immersing a copper coin will convert it into copper sulphate, leaving the wine smelling fine.

Salt and white wine can both stop red wine from staining. Even a deeply coloured wine, such as Barolo, should leave no stain if you dollop on a generous pile of salt, or a splash of white wine, as soon as the wine is spilled.

A peach immersed in Champagne (actually, in any sparkling wine) will soon begin to spin round and round of its own accord. The trick requires rather a large glass – but a smaller downy or hairy fruit (the hairs trap the bubbles), such as a kiwi or gooseberry, will perform to equally entertaining effect. Similarly, a raisin will "swim" up and down the bubble stream of sparkling wine.

Great wine can never be made in stainless steel tanks

Some of the best châteaux in Bordeaux ferment their wine in stainless steel nowadays – and make better wine than ever.

The word "château" indicates quality

It certainly does no such thing – however smart the label. Any wine estate in France can call its building a château (even if it is little smarter than a garden hut) and, in Bordeaux, almost every estate will do so. To complicate matters still further, some co-operatives use a loophole in the rules to put "château" labels on wines they make.

Great wines are never blends; they always come from specific vineyards

What about Champagne like Krug and vintage port, both of which are almost always blends? And what about Grange, the Australian red which has, since its creation in the 1950s, always been a blend from several regions of South Australia?

"Legs" are the sign of a better wine

What the French call the "legs" – and what the Germans call "cathedral windows" – are the streams that flow down the glass once you have swirled the wine around. These are often thought to mean that the wine is especially good. All they really indicate is that the wine is rich in glycerine and was thus made from ripe grapes. Even ripe grapes can be turned into bad wine.

All Rieslings are basically the same grape

The grape of this name grown in Germany and Alsace is the only one of any real quality. When it's grown elsewhere, it is often called the Johannisberg Riesling or the Rhine Riesling to avoid confusion with the completely unrelated and inferior Laski, Welsh and Italico Rizlings. And the grape the Australians used to call the "Hunter Valley Riesling" is actually the Sémillon.

Beaujolais Nouveau has to be drunk by Christmas

There is technically no difference between Beaujolais Nouveau and the kind of Beaujolais we all drink during the rest of the year – except that it is sold earlier. It is usually best drunk quite young, but good Nouveau from one of the region's better producers and vintages can be delicious – and sometimes even better – a year after the harvest.

Screw-top bottles are not as "good" as corked bottles

They are certainly less romantic, but numerous tests have proved that they are far more effective and eliminate the risk of corkiness.

You can always tell a corked wine by smelling the cork

Sometimes a musty-smelling cork will warn you that a wine is faulty; quite often, however, the cork may show no signs of deterioration at all. The sure way to tell a corked wine from a dirty, or otherwise faulty, one is that it will actually smell and taste worse the longer it is in the glass.

All red wines improve with decanting

Some do benefit from the airing they get by being poured from a bottle into a decanter, but less full-bodied wines – such as red Burgundy – can lose some of their fruit by being manhandled in this way.

As a general rule, the only wines that need to be decanted are the ones that have a heavy deposit – all vintage port, most mature red Bordeaux, old Rhônes, Barolos, Australian and Californian reds, for example.

Brut Champagne is bone-dry

It tastes dry; in fact, all Brut Champagnes are slightly sweetened. If you want a bone-dry fizz, go for Brut Zero or Brut Sauvage, which have "zero dosage" – no sweetening at all. But I'll lay money that you'll probably prefer the Brut.

A good vintage in Bordeaux is also good in Burgundy

These two regions are separated the mountain range, the

Many companies make much of the delivery of Beuajolais Nouveau into the shops and bars.

Massif Central, and enjoy completely different climates. In 1982, Bordeaux had a historic vintage for its red wines; Burgundy's reds were pleasant but far from great. Beware too of assuming that vintages are of consistent quality for all the styles produced in a single region. Burgundy's white wines were far better in 1992 than its reds; 1967 Sauternes were wonderful; the red Bordeaux of that year were often little short of appalling.

A hot summer means a good vintage

A cold, rainy summer and autumn will usually make for a bad year, but a hot month of August will not necessarily indicate a good one. Vintages depend on the weather being "right" at various phases of a grape's development, from the spring to the autumn. A late storm at the end of September can spoil what, at the beginning of that month, seemed set to be a great vintage.

Qualitätswein, Appellation Contrôlée, DO, DOC or DOCG on a label are a guarantee of quality

They should be; unfortunately all these expressions legally indicate only that the producer has ensured his wine conforms to a set of controls governing grape varieties, their origin and methods of production – not that he has to be a good wine-maker. Hence they can only really serve as a guide to what the wine is going to be like.

The publishers would like to thank the following sources for their kind permission to reproduce the pictures in this book:

AKG Photo London 8

Bibendum:www.bibendum-wine.co.uk, 113 Regents Park Road
London NW1 8UR, Tel: 020 7916 7706. Email: sales@bibendum-wine.co.uk 91b

Bordeaux Direct: telephone: 0118 903 0311 www.bordeauxdirect.co.uk. 90, 91t

Brown-Forman Wines International 78, 79, 80

Corbis/ Morton Beebe, S.F 29, Michael Boys 34t, Michael Busselle 6, Owen Franken 4b, 4cl, 10, 14, 19, 28b, 67, 72, 83, Robert Holmes 34b, Catherine Karnow 96, Craig Lovell 24, Stephanie Maze 43, Gail Mooney 4r, 4cb, 49, Kelly-Mooney Photography 70, Charles O'Rear 4tc, 5t, 13, 16, 17, 18, 20t, 23, 25, 28t, 32, 35, 36, 37, 38t, 42, 58, 59, 63, 64, 65, 84, 85, 87, 88, 95, Ted Spiegel 9, Jim Sugar Photography 4l, 15t, 21, Ron Watts 20b,

Adam Woolfit 44

Food Features 66, 69

gettyone Stone/Bruce Ayres 71, James Darell 75, David Roth 76

The Image Bank/Felix Clouzot 38b

Portuguese Trade & Tourism Office 30

Sopexa (UK) 33, 40/Jean Pierre Muzard 12, Zvandon, coll.Civa Colman 26

Photos courtesy of ICEX (Spanish Institute for Foreign Trade) 15b

William Taylor 39

Every effort has been made to acknowledge correctly and contact the source and/copyright holder of each picture, and Carlton Books Limited apologises for any unintentional errors or omissions which will be corrected in future editions of this book.

This is a Carlton Book

Text © Robert Joseph 2000
Design and Illustration © Carlton Books Limited

1 3 5 7 9 10 8 6 4 2

This book is sold subject to the condition that it shall not, by way of trade or otherwise, be lent, resold, hired out or otherwise circulated without the publisher's prior written consent in any form of cover or binding other than that in which it is published and without a similar condition, including this condition, being imosed up on the subsequent purchaser.

All rights reserved.

A CIP catalogue for this book is available from the British Library.

ISBN 1 84222 137 X

Project Editor: Vanessa Daubney
Project Art Direction: Brian Flynn
Design and Illustration: Advantage
Production: Lisa French

Printed and bound in Indonesia

THE
Wine Tasting
RECORD

Robert Joseph

Contents

Choosing a Style 6

Storing Wine 10

Serving Wine 13

Wine and Food 16

Tasting Notes 19

Wine Entries

.... 20	 43	
.... 21	 44	
.... 22	 45	
.... 23	 46	
.... 24	 47	
.... 25	 48	
.... 26	 49	
.... 27	 50	
.... 28	 51	
.... 29	 52	
.... 30	 53	
.... 31	 54	
.... 32	 55	
.... 33	 56	
.... 34	 57	
.... 35	 58	
.... 36	 59	
.... 37	 60	
.... 38	 61	
.... 39	 62	
.... 40	 63	
.... 41	 64	
.... 42		

Choosing a Style

Life was easy for Jack Spratt and his wife; each was able to choose the part of the meat he or she liked. Buying a bottle of wine for two can be trickier – especially if one likes red and the other white, or if one has a sweet tooth and the other doesn't. Compromises are not always obviously available. On the other hand, there are now so many different wines on offer – especially in countries like Britain, the USA and Australia, where a semi-ambitious merchant may sell up to 600 styles compared to the dozen or so available in the 1960s – that there is, quite literally, usually something for everybody. The trick lies in deciding on the styles you enjoy, and knowing where to look for them.

Unfortunately, though, many people forget that this is only the first stage. They simply find a wine they like, and stick to it, picking up the same Rioja, Côtes du Rhône or California Chardonnay every time, confident in the knowledge that they know what they are getting – just as there are people who invariably go to the same restaurant and order the same dishes.

Of course, playing safe does have its advantages, but for every occasion when it protects you from disappointment, there are probably at least a couple of times when it'll stop you from discovering a delicious wine – and, quite probably, a bargain.

It's true that the array of wines on offer can be bewildering, but it is possible to group them simplistically by colour, sweetness and body. Indeed this was precisely what British wine-retailers attempted to achieve with a widely adopted coding system for white wines in the 1980s which graded them according to their sweetness – from "1" for a bone-dry Muscadet to "9" for an ultra-sweet Muscat de Beaumes de Venise. At first, traditionalists mumbled and grumbled that one really oughtn't to be categorizing – and thus "demystifying" – wine in this way but, within a very short while, the code became commonplace on bottle labels and shelves.

The success of the white-wine scale, and its popularity among the general public, led inevitably to calls for a similar guide to reds. This proved to be rather more contentious at first, partly because it was suggested that any such innovation might contravene one of the European Union's more arcane regulations. Eventually, however, an A–E scale was widely introduced to give wine-buyers a good idea of whether the wine they were looking at was as lightweight as a Beaujolais or as much of a bruiser as a Barolo. By the mid-1990s, the two scales were thought useful enough by one supermarket for it to group its wines, irrespective of nationality, strictly according to sweetness and price.

Clearly, however, any such codes, by their very nature, inevitably tend both to simplify and to generalize. Some Beaujolais may be a great deal more muscular than others – and there are some middleweight modern Barolos. Although most wines of a particular style or appellation can be fitted into the niche of a single number or letter, there will always be exceptions to prove the rule. Most wine-retailers handle these anomalies by allocating codes to specific wines rather than styles, describing one red Burgundy, for example, as a "B" and another, bigger, one as a "C".

Even so, codes like these can make for odd bedfellows. A New Zealand Sauvignon and a Soave may both be white and similarly dry, but one tastes like over-ripe gooseberries while the other is light, creamy and almondy. A Tavel rosé and a Trocken wine from Germany may, by the same token, taste equally dry, but their flavour is as different as their colour.

Another, more useful, means of grouping wines adopted by merchants is by the grape, or grape varieties, from which they are made. Cabernet Sauvignons and Merlots from coolish vineyards in Bulgaria may indeed be comparable to Bordeaux made from the same varieties. Climate, soil and wine-making styles, however, play such a major part in the flavour of a wine that it can be dangerously misleading to suggest that a trio of Chardonnays – a tropical Australian, semi-sweet Californian and grassy South African, for example – bear any more resemblance than cousins brought up on three different continents.

If you like traditional Bordeaux, the flavour you really enjoy is of a blend of Cabernet Sauvignon, Merlot and Cabernet Franc grapes, coupled with the leanness imposed by a fairly cool climate and made by wine-makers for whom "fruitiness" is not, in any case, a prime consideration. A jammy, blackcurranty Australian Cabernet Sauvignon from, say, the warm Barossa Valley, aged in vanilla-packed, new oak barrels will, on the other hand, probably have more in common with some New-Wave Rioja and Rhônes than with most offerings from the Médoc and St Emilion.

And just to complicate matters a little further, there can be a huge variation in the style and quality of wine-making within even quite small regions: some Australians are making surprisingly lean red wines, while some Bordeaux châteaux are producing wines which taste as though they could have come from the heart of the Napa Valley in California.

To help you through this jungle, I have listed below wines whose flavours are likely to share at least a few discernible characteristics, including them, where appropriate, in more than one group.

Oaky whites
Traditional white Rioja (rare these days)
Graves or Pessac Léognan – new style Bordeaux (France)
Chardonnay – from just about everywhere (though some will be lightly or un-oaked)
Fumé Blanc (California, South Africa, Chile, New Zealand, Australia)
Classy white Burgundy, though how much oak to expect nowadays is impossible to guess (France)
Italian wines with "Barrique" on their labels.

Fresh/grassy whites
Most inexpensive Bordeaux Blanc and young south-west French whites (France)
Sancerre, Pouilly Blanc Fumé (France)
New Zealand Sauvignon Blanc
North German (Mosel, Rheingau) *Trocken*
South German (Scheurebe) Trocken Sauvignon de Touraine (France)
English dry Müller-Thurgau.

Aromatic/spicy whites
Alsace Gewürztraminer (France)
Alsace Tokay-Pinot Gris (France)
Condrieu (France)
Viognier (France, California, Australia, South America)
Arneis (Italy)
Albari (Italy)
Pinot Grigio (Italy)
Grüner Veltliner (Austria)
Viüner Veltliner (Austria)
Rich, unoaked whites
Alsace Pinot Blanc (France)
New Zealand Riesling
Most Mâcon Villages (France)
Trocken Riesling
Alsace Muscat (France)
English dry
Hermitage (France)
Australian Riesling
Graves (old-style) (France)
Gavi (Italy)
Australian Hunter Valley Sémillon
Frascati (Italy).

Dry and off-dry grapey whites
Alsace Riesling (France)
German Kabinett
English medium
German Halbtrocken
Australian dry Muscat
French dry Muscat
Argentinian Torrontes
Portuguese dry Muscat.

Sweet grapey whites
(still and sparkling)
Clairette de Die (France)
Auslese Riesling (Germany, Austria)
Muscat de Beaumes de Venise, Rivesaltes etc. (France)
Moscato d'Asti (Italy)
Moscatel de Setúbal (Portugal)
Alsace Riesling Sélection de Grains Nobles (France)
Moscatel de Valencia (Spain)
Samos Muscat (Greece)
Alsace Muscat Vendange Tardive (France)
Australian Fruity Gordo
Muscat Canelli (California).

Sweet honeyed whites
Sauternes (France)

Moëlleux Vouvray, Quarts de Chaume etc. (France)
Vouvray demi-sec (France)
Jurançon (France)
Ste-Croix-du-Mont (France)
Monbazillac (France)
Orvieto Amabile (Italy)
Late-harvest Sémillon (Australia)
Late-harvest Riesling (Australia, New Zealand, California, South Africa).

Botrytized whites
Alsace Vendange Tardive or Sélection de Grains Nobles (France)
Bonnezeaux (France)
Vouvray Moëlleux/Quarts de Chaume (France)
Barsac or Sauternes (France)
Any "Bunch Select" or "Noble Harvest" wine
German Auslese or Beerenauslese or Trockenbeerenauslese
Edelbeerenlese (Romania)
Hungarian "5 puttonyos" Tokay
Austrian Ausbruch.

Dry sparkling whites
Brut Champagne (France)
Prosecco (Italy)
Crémant de Bourgogne (France)
Cava (Spain)
Blanquette de Limoux (France)
Crémant d'Alsace/Loire (France)
Californian sparkling wine
Australian sparkling wine
New Zealand sparkling wine
South African sparkling wine.

Medium and sweet sparkling wines
(Only if you must; few outside Champagne, Asti and Clairette de Die are good; most are filthy)
Moscato Spumante and Asti (Italy)
Demi-sec Cava (Spain)
Demi-sec and doux or rich Champagne
Demi-sec from just about anywhere
White Lambrusco (Italy)
Sekt (Germany)
Clairette de Die (France).

Dry rosé
Clairet de Bordeaux (France)
Burgundy (France)
Provence (France)
Côtes du Rhône (France)
Rioja (Spain)
Lirac, Tavel (France)
Chiaretto di Bardolino (Italy)
Grenache rosé from California and Australia.

Medium rosé
(Mostly dire)
"Blush" wine from California or just about anywhere else
Portuguese rosé
Rosé d'Anjou (France).

Beaujolais-style/light reds
Alsace Pinot Noir (France)
Sancerre Rouge (light example) (France)
Bourgogne Passetoutgrains (France)
Teroldego Rotaliano (Italy).
Côtes du Rhône Nouveau/Primeur (France)
Dornfelder (Germany)
German Spätburgunder
Gamay from Gaillac, Anjou and Touraine (France)
Lemberger (Washington State)
Gamay and Pinot Noir (Switzerland)
Bardolino (young) (Italy)
Tarrango (Australia)
"Joven" (young) reds from Spain.

Bordeaux-style
Buzet, Chinon, St-Nicolas-de-Bourgueil, Pécharmant (France)
Italian "Super-Tuscans" (such as Ornellaia, Tignanello, etc.)
Californian Cabernet Sauvignon
Château Musar (Lebanon)
Bergerac (France)
Chilean Cabernet Sauvignon and Merlot
Argentinian Cabernet Sauvignon
Australian Cabernet Sauvignon from the cooler regions of Victoria and Western Australia (Margaret River)
New Zealand Cabernet Sauvignon and Merlot
Bulgarian Cabernet Sauvignon/Merlot
Washington State Merlot/Cabernet Sauvignon
Spanish Cabernet Sauvignon
Slovenian Merlot and Cabernet
Italian Merlot/Cabernet
Hungarian Merlot
Vin de Pays d'Oc Merlot and Cabernet Sauvignon (France).

Tough, tannic reds
Traditional Barolo, Barbaresco, Aglianico del Vuture (Italy)
Cahors (France) – though only old-fashioned examples
Traditional Hermitage and Cornas (France)
St-Estèphe (France)
Douro (Portugal)
Priorato (Spain)
Bigger Californian Zinfandel
Some Australian Shiraz
South African Merlot, Cabernet, Pinotage.

Rustic reds
Corvo, Taurasi, Montepulciano d'Abruzzo (Italy)
Cahors, Corbières/Fitou/Minervois (France)
Dão (Portugal)
Bulgarian "Country Reds"
Valdepean "Country Reds"
inervSouth African Pinotage.

Sweet and off-dry reds
Piat d'Or (France)
Recioto di Valpolicella (Italy)
Lambrusco (Italy)
Some Crimean reds
Romanian Pinot Noir.

Burgundy-style
Older cru Beaujolais (France)
Oregon and Californian Pinot Noir
Bouzy Rouge (France)
Antipodean Pinot Noir
Chilean Pinot Noir
South African Pinot Noir
St Laurent (Austria)
Dry Romanian Pinot Noir.

Rich and raisiny
Málaga (Spain)
Recioto di Valpolicella (Italy)
Malmsey Madeira (Portugal)
Mavrodaphne (Greece)
Marsala (Italy)
Australian Liqueur Muscat and Tokay
Commandaria (Cyprus)
Pedro Ximénez sherry (Spain).

Medium-bodied spicy reds
Côtes du Rhône, Crozes Hermitage, St-Joseph,
Vin de Pays d'Oc Syrah (France)
Nebbiolo d'Alba (Italy)
Lighter-bodied Zinfandel (California)
Medium-bodied South African Pinotage
Chilean or Argentinan Malbec
Château Musar (Lebanon)
South African Pinotage.

Fuller-bodied spicy reds
Côte Rôtie, Cornas, Hermitage (France)
Argentinian or Australian Malbec.
Petit Verdot from anywhere.
Fuller-bodied South African Pinotage
Australian Shiraz/Cabernet, Shiraz, Grenache,
and warmer-climate Cabernet (e.g. Barossa)
Californian Syrah, Grenache, Zinfandel
Modern Barolo (Italy)
Priorato (Spain).

Sherry-like wines
Vin Santo (Italy)
Sercial Madeira (Portugal)
Montilla (Spain)
Vin jaune (France).

Port-like wines
Banyuls (France)
Recioto della Valpolicella, Anghelu Ruju (Italy)
Commandaria (Cyprus)
New-World "Port".

NEW WORLD OR NEW WAVE

In the late 1980s, as they became increasingly and uncomfortably aware of growing competition from wines made on the other side of the world, producers in France in particular began to distinguish between what they considered the "simple" wines of the New World – which, as they saw it, were merely the produce of single grape varieties grown in warm regions – and the more complex, finer fare from Old-World vineyards with the classic "terroir" qualities of soil and climate.

At first, these traditionalists had a point; quite soon, however, their apartheid-like division of the world between the New and the Old lost its relevance as Frenchmen increasingly took to making wine in countries like Chile, New Zealand and California, while pioneering, native-born wine-makers of these and other New-World countries themselves developed new cooler regions and styles which were completely different from the fruit-and-oak cocktails with which they had been associated a few years earlier.

By 1995, New-World producers had developed wines with such Old-World-style complexity that a chagrined team of France's top tasters were unable to tell several of them from examples hailing from some of the most distinguished vineyards in Bordeaux and Burgundy.

More to the point, though, than what one might call the "Europeanization" of New-World wines, was the "Californianization" of some of the Old-World classics. Just as hamburgers and shopping malls made their inexorable way into Florence, Bordeaux and Barcelona, wine-makers consciously or unconsciously adapted their wine-making to suit Anglo-Saxon wine critics and the more "international" palate over which they held sway. New oak barrels, ripe fruit flavours and "soft tannins" became the order of the day on a number of Old-World estates which, unsurprisingly perhaps, were swiftly rewarded by acclaim and orders.

Meanwhile, increasing numbers of dynamic producers in previously overlooked regions of the Old World such as Languedoc Roussillon in France, Navarra in Spain and – to a lesser extent – areas in southern Italy, also turned their hands successfully, with or without the help of New-World wine-makers and consultants, to competing with the oaky varietal wines of Australia and California.

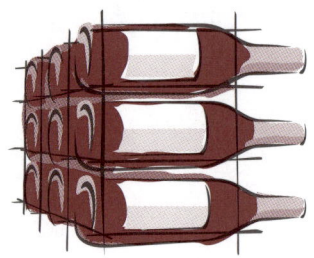

Storing Wine

The question of where and how to store wine is, like the puzzle of where you mislaid your mobile phone, how to collect your e-mail while travelling and recording the right programme off your television, an essentially modern complaint. One hundred years ago, while the wealthy had cellars full of fine bottles, they were a small minority; most people simply bought their red wine – and it usually was red – in much the same way as they might milk – drinking it in the few days, weeks or months before it went off. If you were to have taken a look at the contents of the cellars that did exist, you'd have found a tiny range of regions and styles – compared to the plethora available today.

The mass of bottles on offer now though share one thing in common, however: they'll all be full of relatively young wine. Today, while you can pick up an old movie or book in a local shop or over the Net, classic, mature bottles of wine are a lot harder to find. Indeed, buying wines from harvests as recently as five years or so ago can be as tricky as a first edition of last year's best-selling novel. A few merchants and producers helpfully do hold onto older vintages – and sell them at appropriately high prices – but the majority now market their wines in much the same way as a boutique would sell its clothes: proudly announcing the arrival of a new vintage as though it were a designer's latest collection.

So, if you like drinking mature wine and you don't want to do your shopping at auction, you'd be well advised to begin to set aside a few bottles right now for future drinking. But where are you going to put them? And how are you going to ensure that their contents mature in the ideal conditions? After all, there's no point in proudly pulling out a dusty Bordeaux or Burgundy you bought a decade ago for your dinner guests if it has turned to vinegar.

To judge by some of the so-called "wine collectors" about whom one can regularly read in the glossier American wine magazines, the answer lies in creating a Bluebeard's palace in which to stash your hoard. Even the owners of more modest collections sometimes fall into the trap of imagining that the flashiness of the storing system somehow reflects the seriousness of the wines. Expensive, glass-fronted, refrigerated cabinets or shelving with mahogany doors often have more to do with impressing visitors than appropriate storage.

Of course, people lucky enough to have several thousand bottles of priceless old claret would be foolish if they did not make the effort to keep them in the best conditions possible, but that's not to say that they – or anyone else – have to throw unlimited amounts of money at the problem.

So, let's look at the kind of storage conditions a wine ideally needs. First, there's the temperature. 7-10°C would be optimum – about as cool as you'd want to drink your white wines. Below 5° is risky, as light, low-alcohol, wines can freeze at this kind of temperature and force their corks out of the bottle. Anything above 20-25° will risk cooking off some of the more delicate characteristics, particularly of older and more delicate wines. As a general rule, the cooler the environment, the more slowly the wine will mature. Like people who carelessly expose their skin to extreme sunlight, wines stored in a warm place tend to show the effects of age rather more rapidly.

Whatever the average temperature of your storage area, though, the crucial thing is to keep it as constant as possible. A wine will suffer more from a daily switchback ride from 15° to 20° than from a steady 20–22°. Which is why the average kitchen with its violent changes in temperature is just about the worst place you could choose to keep your most treasured bottles. Thermometers which show variations are inexpensive and well-worth buying.

After temperature, the next concern is humidity. The cork that protects the wine from the outside world is as much a piece of wood as any piece of furniture. If you keep your Victorian table in a dry, centrally-heated environment, it will crack and warp. If you do the same to a cork, it will shrink and allow the liquid to escape and air to enter the bottle. Storing the bottles on their sides ensures that one end of the cork remains moist, but it provides no such benefit for the other end – the one you are going to attack with your corkscrew. So, the place you keep your wine should be fairly humid. If you need to make a dry place a little damper, you can use a humidifier – or a sponge in a bowl of water. The only drawback to a really humid cellar lies in the risk of labels being spoiled or even falling off the bottles completely. One way to avoid this is to spray them with protective laquer – or with hairspray.

Light may be good for plants, but it's bad for wine – which is why, apart from Sauternes, most reds and whites come in green or – more rarely – brown glass bottles. So, the place you store your wine should be dark. The effects of vibration on wine are less well established. Many London wine merchants traditionally had few worries about storing their finest claret in arches beneath railway lines, but there is evidence that a tranquil environment will slow the ageing process.

Smells are another matter. While the cork and capsule are supposed to protect wine from the environment surrounding the bottle, on occasion unpleasant aromas in cellars do seem to get past this barrier. Wines from cellars in which a drain pipe has broken or where there has been smoke from a fire have been spoiled – as, possibly, have wines from cellars that are simply musty. So, you should ensure that there is enough ventilation to keep the air smelling fresh.

So, there you have it: what you need is a place that's constantly cool, dark, damp, and free from vibration and smells. If you are lucky enough to live in a house with a purpose-built cellar, that's probably precisely what you've got beneath your feet. If, however, like most of us, the place you hang your hat is an appartment or a house with no basement, well, you're going to have to think a little more laterally. Is there a cupboard or a fireplace, perhaps that could be converted into a cellar? Maybe you could insulate a loft. If you have a garage or a garden, you might be able to excavate a cellar there (think of all those nuclear bunkers that were dug into the earth by worried people in the worst days of the Cold War). You could buy a wine-cellar kit which you can even sink into the floor of your kitchen (provided you don't have neighbours below). Alternatively, you might invest in one of the growing range of purpose-built temperature-controlled wine-cupboards. These devices which are in fact little more than fancy refrigerators with a special thermostat work well, but don't come cheap – which explains why some resourceful wine lovers have been known to do their own fridge-conversions.

If space is really tight, you could follow my example in a previous home, by hanging wine racks on the walls above the doorframes of a narrow corridor. This, though, was a fairly desperate measure which, given my own and my friends' thin-bloodedness and the tendency of heat to rise, was far less than ideal for wine. In situations like this, you might be best to store your best wine elsewhere – in a friend's cellar, with the merchant from whom you bought it, or in the cellars of a specialist wine-storage company. Quite apart from ensuring that the bottles are being well-kept, this has the advantage of reducing the temptation to drink them prematurely. However, wherever you store your wine, don't forget that it is one of your more valuable possessions. So check your insurance – and make sure that it keeps up with the likely rise in value of your bottles over the years. And, if entrusting wine to other people, beware of the disaster that befell a friend of mine whose best bottles innocently ended up as part of an acrimonious custody battle between a couple when their marriage fell apart. To avoid this kind of situation – or arguments with bailifs collecting debts that have nothing to do with you – it is worth labelling your bottles and cases with your name.

Once you have found the place or places in which you are going to store your wine, the next task lies in deciding what you are going to put in it and how you are going to arrange the bottles. Racks – wooden, plastic or metal – are the ideal way to store individual bottles. Wooden self-assembly and folding racks are inexpensive and readily obtainable. Models which have sharp metal edges tend to tear labels as bottles are being inserted or removed, but they are inexpensive and have the advantage of fitting into tricky areas. Indeed, they can be cut to shape and are sold on a per-hole basis. If you buy purpose-made racks, bear in mind, though, that they are not generally suited to half-bottles, magnums and larger bottles, so remember to make

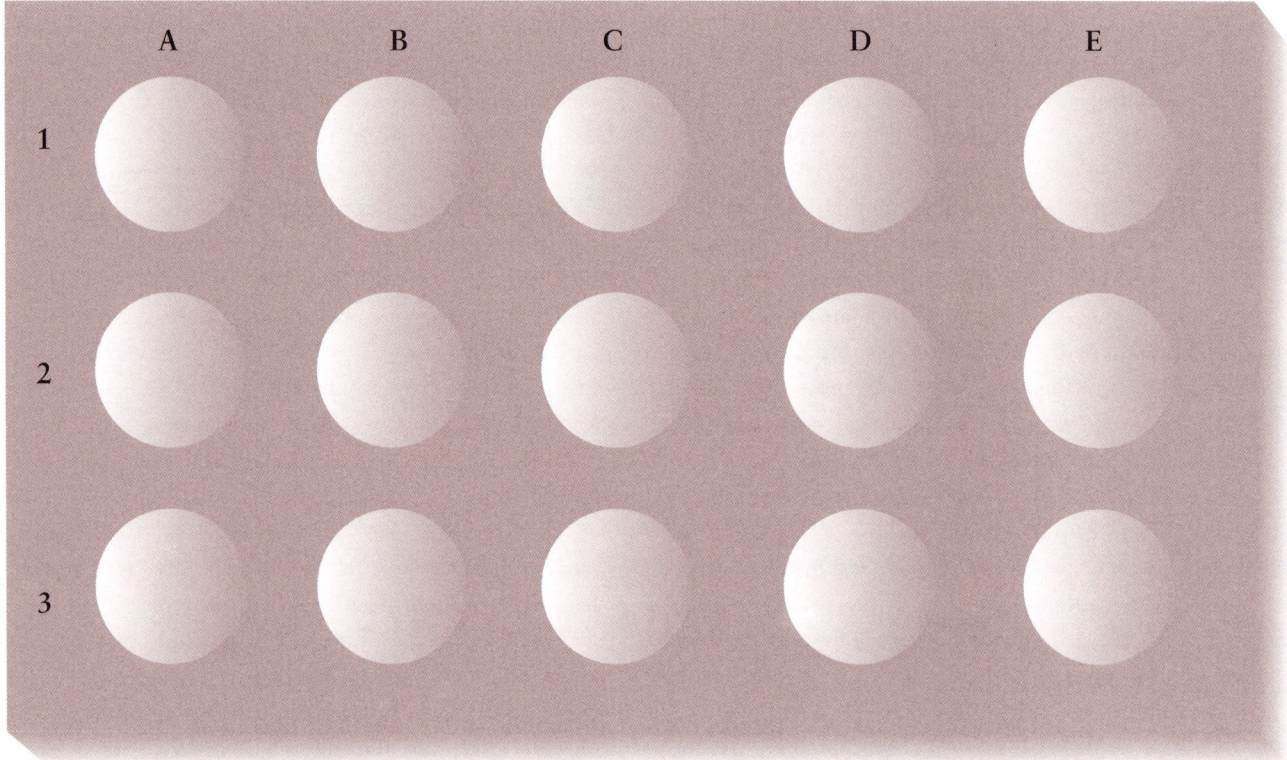

A simple racking system where holes are labelled A–Z horizontally and 1, 2, 3, etc. vertically.

space for these if you are likely to need to store them.

Handier folk can, given the space, build bin-units using wooden shelving, chimney pipe or breeze blocks in which several bottles of the same wine can be kept in a pile. These are perfect for wines you buy by the case, but are less handy if, like me, you like picking up one or two bottles at a time. It can be rather tedious emptying a bin to reach the bottle at the bottom – but rather wiser than trying to pull it out from beneath the others.

Laying out a Wine Cellar

It is useful to be able to attach cards with numbers or wine names to the bin or rack so that unnecessary searching is reduced to a minimum. Leave space for these. One of the advantages of racks is that they facilitate keeping track of your wines – especially if you use my system for dispersing the bottles. Instead of allocating specific parts of the rack to particular styles (which always proves problematical when your stock of Loire reds, for example, outgrows its corner) you adopt the principal of the computer spreadsheet, giving each hole in the rack its own identity. Holes are lettered horizontally (from A–Z; AA–ZZ and so on) and given numbers vertically. As new wines arrive, they go into any available holes; all you have to do is record the fact that your four prized bottles of 1988 Château Latour, for example, are in B34, E12, K51 and L2 while the Bulgarian red you'd set aside for the casserole is at A23.

If this system works admirably for wines you are almost certain that you are going to drink, cases of claret you may want to resell at auction should be kept in their original wooden boxes. Doing this will help you to get the highest possible price under the hammer. Beware, though, of any wine in cardboard boxes – however sturdy they appear. If your cellar is as humid as it ought to be, there's a strong risk of them falling apart and spilling bottles all over the floor. Which brings me to my final hint: one for which you might one day be very grateful. If you are lucky enough to have a real cellar, cover the floor in fine gravel. It provides a remarkably soft landing for any bottles that slip through your fingers.

Serving Wine

Wine can be an etiquette minefield, in which otherwise confident adults seem to imagine that if the port were to be passed the wrong way, or a red opened before a white, or poured into the wrong kind of glass, the sky would fall in on their guests.

Well, I'll leave this and just about every other social dilemma to Debrett's and concentrate instead on offering a set of simple (and by no means hard and fast) rules which should allow you to relax and relish each and every bottle of wine you open at its best.

UNCORKING

The best corkscrew by far is the American Screwpull. Any other types should be formed like a spiral, rather than the screw after which they are named. The device with two flat prongs rather than a screw or spiral is either called an "Ah So" because of its purported ease of use, or "Butler's Friend", because it supposedly allowed deceitful servants to appropriate a glass or two of wine, top the bottle up with water and replace the undamaged cork without detection. The trick of using it – sliding the prongs down between cork and bottle, then pressing them together as you draw the cork – takes a bit of mastering: practise on an already-opened and recorked bottle.

Ironically, the tool which no traditional cellar or sommelier once lacked, a knife to cut the foil, or a "foil cutter", is much more necessary today than it ever was in the past, now that tinfoil and infuriatingly shrink-fitted plastic have replaced the easily peelable – but medically suspect – lead capsule.

DECANTING

There's a great deal of nonsense talked about the importance of letting a wine "breathe" – and a fair bit of sense too. In fact, the principal reason for decanting wine, or port, should be to remove sediment, which many wines – Rioja and red Burgundy, for example – do not have. So why decant a wine with no sediment? Well, what you are doing is, in effect, letting it get its act together before it hits your and your guests' glasses. Wines which appear "dumb" or "closed" may open up with a little time in the decanter; others with a lot of tannin (for example, claret, Barolo, many Californian Cabernets and most Portuguese reds) can certainly benefit from being decanted – or at least uncorked and simply left open for a while before they are drunk. Rather astringent cheaper wines may soften up too and, surprisingly to many people, plenty of classy white wines such as young white Burgundy and top class New World Chardonnay reveal their qualities after being poured into a decanter

On the other hand, some wines are somewhat short of an act to get together; young flavourless reds and venerable bottles which have lost their fruit over the years in the rack are going to gain no more from a period of enforced breathing than an eight-stone weakling or an ailing 70-year-old might benefit from an enforced cross-country run. Remember that decanting can be an unsettling procedure. Some more delicate wines, such as mature red Burgundy, can be quite spoiled by decanting.

But assuming the wine is worth decanting, how do you do it? For the nervous, muslin or a coffee filter paper will effectively separate sediment from liquid; for the steadier of hand, a candle flame, a torch or a piece of white card held just behind the neck of the bottle should enable you to see when the trickle of transparent wine begins to become thicker sludge. Be certain not to shake up the bottle before decanting and pour slowly, keeping the flow constant. And, if you don't have a decanter, don't worry. All you have to do is decant the wine carefully into a jug before pouring it back into its original bottle (which you have rinsed out with water).

GLASSES

There's no doubt that a beautifully made and shaped glass can make the drinking of a finer wine seem just that bit more special than simply slugging it down from a beaker – even Keats's "beaker full of the warm South".

Certain glass shapes are by tradition associated with certain types of wine – but remember that this, again, is only tradition, not law. Moreover, some of these traditions are actually bad for the wine. The saucer-shaped Champagne glass will make your fizz as flat as a pancake, while a Jerezano would be appalled by the thought that the delicate aromas of his elegant fino sherry were destined to evaporate from the brimming surface of a tiny, overfilled "schooner". On the other hand, an enterprising Austrian manufacturer called Georg Riedel has recently produced a growing number of individual glasses that genuinely do bring out the best characteristics in all sorts of wine styles. Only the most devoted collector would invest the considerable sums required for a complete set of Riedel glasses, but any enthusiast would welcome the chance to own a few examples from the range.

If you haven't got the "right" shape of glass, make sure the one you have got is smaller at the rim than across the bowl, which will prevent the bouquet of the wine from escaping. Whatever the wine and whatever the glass, don't over-pour. A third to half full is just about right.

ORDER

There exists a set of principles which dictate the most sensible order in which wines should be served during the course of a meal. Basically they are: white before red; dry before sweet; light before heavy; young before old; ordinary before fine. The underlying aim is to lead your palate gently up the scale of increasing fullness, "flavoursomeness" and quality, rather than swinging wildly between styles.

But it's sometimes impossible to observe one of these rules without breaking another – so check against the rest of the list. The more that "agree", the better; a mature, full California Chardonnay can safely follow a young, light Beaujolais, for example, even though this breaks the white/red rule.

It's a good idea anyway to make sure there is a jug or bottle of water on the table, so that palates can be cleansed and refreshed between wines.

TEMPERATURE

For reds, the word *chambré* – meaning at room temperature – is rather misleading. Which room? What temperature? Supposedly "standard" conditions can vary a great deal. Remember that a century ago, when the French coined the term *chambré*, even the wealthiest of wine-drinkers lived in homes that were far less warm than our centrally-heated cocoons. To them "room temperature" often meant only a few degrees warmer than the cellar from which the wine was brought.

But not all reds are the same. Served too warm, even the finest red wine can seem heavy and rather dull. In fact, some red wines are best drunk slightly chilled – fresh, fruity Beaujolais and light red Loires desperately need to be served at temperatures only slightly higher than that at which you would serve a white Burgundy.

What about chilling wine? If you are unfortunate enough to have to give your guests a truly unpalatable red, white or pink wine, bear in mind that the colder any food or drink, the less one can taste it. Chilled heavily enough, Coca-Cola would be almost indistinguishable from sweet Champagne.

Sweet wines such as Sauternes and Muscat de Beaumes de Venise can just about take being served almost vodka-cold, though they deserve rather gentler treatment; dry ones, particularly richer wines like white Burgundy and older New-World Sémillon, need far gentler handling. Indeed, the best of these are at their best a degree or two warmer than some lighter-bodied reds.

If you're chilling in a hurry, an ice bucket filled with cold water and generous handfuls of ice cubes is far more successful than ice alone – and so much easier to get the bottle back into. Serve only small portions at first to allow the rest of the wine to cool down further. If you need to warm a wine up, stand it in a bucket of tepid water for 10 minutes.

Serving Temperatures

The figures given for the following wine styles are approximate, but if you really want to be precise, you could use one of the floppy plastic thermometers which, though intended for recalcitrant children's foreheads, will wrap round and adhere to the neck of a bottle very satisfactorily.

Red Wine

The tougher and more tannic a wine, the more it will benefit from being served a little warmer, while younger, fruitier reds will be best at a lower temperature

- Chill lightly (10–13°C, or no more than an hour in the door of the fridge): Beaujolais – but not the crus (Fleurie, Morgon etc.); red Loire (Gamay, Pinot Noir and Cabernet); young French *vins de pays*; young Bardolino and Valpolicella and Vino Joven – young, unoaked – reds from Spain.

- "Room temperature" (14–16°C, which is actually rather cooler than most living rooms; your wine should certainly not be stored anywhere warmer than this, and if you are bringing it up from a chilly cellar it may need a little standing time):
Most other reds, particularly younger red Burgundy and Rhônes and older Bordeaux, Pinot Noirs from the New World, Chianti, younger Rioja, New-World Grenache and Pinotage from South Africa.

- Open at least an hour before serving and serve a little warmer (16–18°C):
Older Burgundy; younger, more tannic Bordeaux and Rhônes; Californian Zinfandel, bigger New-World Cabernet Sauvignon, Merlot and Shiraz; Barolo, and other bigger Italian reds, older Rioja and wines from Ribera del Duero.

- Decant an hour or so before serving:
Young claret; heavy Portuguese reds; bigger Italians such as Barolo and Barbaresco (though older ones should be decanted just before the meal); Australian Shiraz.

Rosé

Chill, but don't over-chill, particularly if the wine is dry; two hours in the door of the fridge or 5–10 minutes in a bucket of ice and water is ample.

White Wine

The rule here is to weigh up the concentration of aroma and flavour of the wine, its age and the richness of its texture. The lower the temperature, the less a wine will smell and the less evident any richness it may have.

- Serve coldest – around 4–8°C – a good two or three hours in the fridge or 10–15 minutes in a bucket of ice and water:
Lighter sweeter wines such as Rieslings from Germany, dessert and the more everyday sparkling wines..

- A little less cool (8–11°C):
Most fuller-bodied, drier and semi-dry whites and Champagne, along with bigger, more complex dessert wines such as Sauternes and Beerenauslese wines from Germany; aromatic wines such as Arneis from Italy, Viognier from the Rhône and the New World and Gewürztraminer; younger simpler Sauvignons and Chardonnays from just about everywhere.

- Around 12–13°C – about an hour in the fridge door. Or 5–10 minutes in a bucket of ice and water:
Richer dry wines such as Burgundy, Alsace, traditional white Rioja; bigger, more complex Sauvignons, Sémillons and New-World Chardonnays.

Wine and Food

"You can't possibly wear that shirt with that jacket!" "How could you even dream of drinking a white wine with meat?" The business of putting together foods and wines, like that of choosing clothes or furnishing fabrics, is full of rules and traps for the unwary which can be so daunting that one could be forgiven for dismissing them all and eating and drinking what you like. After all, a full-flavoured New-World Chardonnay could be perfect with all sorts of meat dishes and Burgundians traditionally poach trout in red wine. Some of the traps are real though – like orange ties against green shirts, sardines and claret taken together taste downright nasty – and some of the rules, provided they are not taken too seriously, can be quite handy.

It is worth bearing in mind the style of food a wine was originally intended to partner – usually the dishes enjoyed in the region where the wine was made. A wine like Barolo, for example, was never made to be drunk with a plateful (or rather half-full) of dainty *nouvelle cuisine* morsels – any more than Sauternes was intended to be served with grilled sole.

But today, people, dishes and wines travel far more widely than ever before. A London or New York dinner party might easily include dishes from three different countries – and wines from three more. And some unexpected partnerships of flavour and style can be the most successful of all.

There are three kinds of relationship between food and wine. There are the personality clashes, in which each brings out the worst in the other. Try drinking red Burgundy with a plateful of oily sardines, or with a grapefruit, and you will know exactly what I mean. At the other end of the scale, there is the love-at-first-sight relationship which, like a bowlful of strawberries and cream, tastes magically better and somehow quite different to either ingredient taken by itself.

Between the two, there is the great mass of food and wine pairings in which the two rub along well enough, never actively clashing, but not doing an awful lot for each other either.

And, finally, there are the handy "bridges", the components which can bring otherwise incompatible flavours together. Try a tannic claret with a rare piece of beef and you will probably find that the meat makes the wine taste tougher. Now add a touch of mustard and have another taste. Astonishingly, the combination of the three flavours disarms that toughness completely.

The key to discovering partnerships that work lies in understanding the weight as well as the type of flavours you are dealing with – plus a helping of courage. Brave were the souls who first discovered how delicious game with chocolate, or a little pepper sprinkled over fresh strawberries could be.

DESSERT WINES

According to some rule books all desserts deserve Sauternes – except those which involve chocolate or ginger, both of which are believed to be incompatible with any wine. But

Matching ~ Wine with Food

WINE FOR FISH

To avoid the nasty metallic taste that you get when you drink red wine with fish, the trick is to choose the right wine for the right fish. Oily ones like sardines need crisp dry whites – such as Vinho Verde or Muscadet.

SALMON

Subtle poached salmon needs white wine without too much acidity. Lighter-bodied Chardonnay such as Mâcon-Villages can be ideal – as can good Soave, Frascati or white Châteauneuf-du-Pape. If you must have a red (perhaps because one wine has to accompany both meat and fish), modern (possibly New World) Pinot Noir can be ideal. Smoked salmon is said to go well with Alsace Gewürztraminer; I prefer another Alsace – Tokay-Pinot Gris – or white Hermitage.

SEAFOOD

Oysters call for bone-dry whites – Muscadet, Sancerre, Chablis or Verdicchio. For scallops, try slightly richer wines such as lighter Italian Chardonnays or Pinot Bianco – and lobster can be perfect with, again, Tokay-Pinot Gris from Alsace.

GRILLED FISH

Sea bass and river fish such as trout go well with Chardonnay – particularly southern Burgundies such as St-Véran, as well as oaky white Rioja (particularly Monopole) or top-class Soave (try Pieropan's version). Dry German or Australian Riesling is perfect with turbot.

WINE FOR POULTRY & GAME

CHICKEN AND TURKEY

Avoid too strong or too subtle a wine with these; simply cooked dishes go well with light reds (Beaujolais or red Loire, for example). For a white to accompany plainly roasted poultry, try a Chardonnay or an Alsace or German Riesling. Creamy chicken dishes need the acid bite of dry, fruity Sauvignon (from New Zealand), good dry Vouvray or Alsace Riesling.

DUCK

Roast duck can be as delicious with fruity wines as with fruity sauces. Try Beaujolais, blackcurranty Cabernet Sauvignon from Chile, a red Loire or a light claret.

GAME BIRDS

The gamier the meat, the spicier the wine must be. So, for subtler game birds, try Bordeaux from St Emilion and Pomerol or a red Burgundy. For stronger-flavoured meat, go for northern Rhône reds such as Crozes Hermitage, St-Joseph, Hermitage or Côte Rôtie, Australian Shiraz or Californian Zinfandel.

VENISON AND RABBIT

The strong flavours of venison are best matched by spicy French wines such as Cahors, Madiran, Hermitage and Châteauneuf, Barolo from Italy, Australian Shiraz-Cabernet and Californian Zinfandel and Cabernet. With rabbit or hare, serve old-fashioned, country-style wines such as Italian Barbera and Chianti, or Bairrada and Douro from Portugal.

WINE FOR MEAT

Tradition dictates that red meat calls for red wine, but the kind of red wine depends on the type of meat and the sauce in which it has been prepared. If the sauce has been made with a wine from a particular region, there is an argument for serving it with a wine from the same region. A creamy sauce, however, needs a soft wine with plenty of fresh, fruity acidity to cut through the richness – say, a good Beaujolais or a Bardolino from Italy. A rich, meaty casserole requires heartier wines such as Châteauneuf-du-Pape, Californian Zinfandel, Australian Shiraz or Grenache, Barolo, a rich Burgundy, such as Gevrey Chambertin, or a Bordeaux from St Emilion. Roast beef and steaks prepared without sauce go well with Burgundy, Rioja, richer cru Beaujolais, Chianti, or lighter Zinfandels from California, but – surprisingly – less successfully with Bordeaux and other Cabernet Sauvignon. The tannin in these wines seems to be accentuated by the meat.

Adding mustard, though, for some reason usually reduces this effect. Cabernet-based wines are better with lamb, however, which is why traditionalists like to eat it with Bordeaux from Pauillac. This is a meat that also teams well with a rich red from Rioja, Languedoc Roussillon or Provence. Pork can be paired equally well with red or white wines. For white, try a rich Chardonnay, a traditional Rioja, a Tokay-Pinot Gris or a Pinot Blanc from Alsace, or a drier Riesling from Germany. If you prefer red, then go for a medium-bodied wine such as a Dolcetto, a Valpolicella or Chianti, a red Loire or a Beaujolais.

FOREIGN FLAVOURS

In some parts of the world, such as India and China, wine has no traditional place at all. Consequently, their cuisine can offer something of a challenge when it comes to selecting wine.

Some curries are so dominated by the flavour of peppers and spice that it is certainly not worth choosing a top-quality wine. But if you must have wine, try fresh fruity or warm spicy styles, such as chilled young Beaujolais, red Loire, young Rhône or Australian Shiraz, dry German Riesling – or a fruity, off-dry rosé such as Mateus. For milder curries try Dolcetto, Valpolicella or Bairrada, while creamy dishes are well-matched with Sauvignon.

Creole, Chinese and Thai food often combine so many sweet, sour and savoury flavours that it is best to go for a very tasty wine. My favourite is New Zealand Sauvignon Blanc, but Alsace Gewürztraminer and drier southern French rosés are lovely – as is chilled Asti. The same rules apply to Japanese food, though saké– rice wine, which is usually drunk warm – is more traditional.

while, at its most spicy, ginger overpowers almost any other flavour, at its mildest, it can match late-harvest Gewürztraminer.

Chocolate can be lovely with Australian or Californian Orange Muscats or, surprisingly, with rich, fruity Cabernet Sauvignon from California. Fresh fruit tarts and mousses need fruity wines. A sweet Riesling (such as German Auslese) or Muscat (a late-harvest Alsace, a Beaumes de Venise from the Rhône, or a Moscatel de Setúbal from Portugal) can be perfect.

Creamy desserts, such as syllabub and crème brulée, are better served by sweet wines from the Loire, like Vouvray Moëlleux, or by Sauternes.

Very sweet desserts such as baked or steamed sponge puddings will overpower all but the most intense of wines. You could try Hungarian Tokay, Malmsey or Bual Madeira, or my favourite: Liqueur Muscat or Tokay from Australia.

WINE FOR CHEESE

Red wine is not as perfect a partner for cheese as most people imagine; in fact, white wine can be far better – especially with high-fat cheeses. One way to get over this is to follow the Iberian tradition of serving quince jelly or some other kind of jam with the cheese. This also seems to work as a bridge between blue cheese and red wine – a combination that can otherwise be very nasty indeed.

Dutch cheeses and goat's cheese are delicious with Sancerre or Pouilly Blanc Fumé, though New Zealand Sauvignon Blanc and Chablis can be successful too.

One of the great wine-and-cheese partnerships is Roquefort and Sauternes. The combination of honeyed sweetness and salty tang is perfect, but you can swap the Roquefort for any similar blue cheese and replace the Sauternes with a late-harvest Riesling or even a moëlleux wine from the Loire.

Soft French cheeses are made for gentle, fruity red Burgundy. Cheddar can go with Bordeaux – in particular, examples made primarily from the rich-flavoured Merlot grape – but I would opt for port (vintage or tawny) or Madeira. And don't forget Stilton and port.

Tasting Notes

Welcome to your part of the book – to the record you are going to keep, not only of the whereabouts of particular bottles, but of when and where you bought them, the people you drank them with, the dishes they accompanied and the way they were received. Whether or not you keep any other kind of diary, I can almost guarantee that the pages of this book will provide a unique source of memories in years to come. But they will do a lot more than that. The record will, if used carefully, teach you an enormous amount about the way particular wines behave and evolve – and about your own and your friends' tastes. And how they too can evolve over the years.

Wine is after all – or certainly should be – inextricably associated with companionship. When you pull the cork on a bottle whose details are worth noting down, the chances are that you'll be drinking it with food and with at least one other person. The occasion might be a dinner party, an anniversary, a romantic evening – or an attempt to build bridges with the boss or bank manager. You may be enjoying – or on occasion, unfortunately not enjoying – your first ever experience of a particular wine or vintage. Or you may be drinking a wine you haven't tasted for a while. Do you agree with the verdict the critics gave it? How has it changed? Is it maturing attractively? Has it still some way to go before it's at its best? Or is it flatter and duller than you remember it to have been? Have you left it in the rack for too long? Should you (or maybe shouldn't you) have decanted it? Maybe it needed a little longer (or less time) to breathe before serving – or to be served slightly cooler (or warmer).

The record will also serve as the equivalent of the race-goer's form-book. Patterns will emerge: particular vintages will display common characteristics (allowing you, for example to decide that it is – or isn't – time to start drinking the '98 Bordeaux) and some producers (in Burgundy, for instance) may prove to offer more reliable quality than others.

There are practical considerations too. Where did you buy the wine? And for how much? And what might it be worth now if you were to buy (or sell) it at auction? As you leaf through the pages, does one merchant seem to have provided better wines – or better value?

And how did the wine go with the food? Books – including this one – recommend all sorts of marriages of food and wine, but they can be little surer of their matchmaking than an astrololger who suggests that Librans ought to be compatible with people born under the sign of Aquarius. One producer's dry Vouvray may be far drier than another's – and will go with quite different dishes. An oaky Australian Chardonnay might be better with smoked salmon – and less good with plainly cooked cod – than one that has never seen the inside of a barrel. No food-and-wine guide can ever accommodate aspects of vinous character that may only become apparent once the wine has been poured. Age can also have an enormous influence on the way a wine performs with food. A Burgundy that stood up to a sneeze-inducing steak au poivre in its fruity youth may eventually soften so much with age that it will be overwhelmed by a coq au vin.

Finally, of course, there are the other people. The question of which guests warrant the best bottles is one that inevitably vexes many wine enthusiasts – especially when they discover that the Bordeaux they bought for £10 a few years ago is now worth £200. All too often, wines like these are left to gather thicker layers of dust until the "appropriate" gathering of fine and experienced palates can be gathered to share the experience of opening it. As a writer who has been lucky and privileged enough over the years to have tasted enormous numbers of great wines, I admit that there is no fun to be had in watching a wonderful, irreplaceable claret being knocked back as though it were Coca-Cola. On the other hand, I've never forgotten Eric de Rothschild, the owner of Château Lafite, once making the point that the best and most generous thing for anyone who loves wine to do is to pass that love and enthusiasm onto someone else – by offering them a taste of something really good. And when you do that, don't forget to record the occasion in this book – because, with any luck you'll be mentioning the way that friend appreciated other wine on all sorts of other occasions.

Wine

Bottles to be found in hole/s:

Price　　　　　　　　　　Date　　　　　　　　　　Number of bottles bought:

Grape　　　　　　　　　　Region　　　　　　　　　Vintage

Producer　　　　　　　　　　　　　　　　　　　　Country

Purchased from

Critical comment

Affix label

Date opened

Served with

Guests

Comments

Mark

Wine

Bottles to be found in hole/s: Number of bottles bought:

Price   Date   Vintage

Grape   Region   Country

Producer

Purchased from

Critical comment

Date opened

Served with

Affix label

Guests

Comments

Mark

Wine

Bottles to be found in hole/s: Number of bottles bought:

Price   Date   Vintage

Grape   Region   Country

Producer

Purchased from

Critical comment

Affix label   Date opened

                                                                 Served with

                                                                 Guests

                                                                 Comments

                                                                 Mark

Wine

Bottles to be found in hole/s: Number of bottles bought:

Price   Date   Vintage

Grape   Region   Country

Producer

Purchased from

Critical comment

Date opened   *Affix label*

Served with

Guests

Comments

Mark

Wine

Bottles to be found in hole/s:

Number of bottles bought:

Price　　　　　　　　Date

Vintage

Grape　　　　　　　　Region

Country

Producer

Purchased from

Critical comment

Affix label

Date opened

Served with

Guests

Comments

Mark

Wine

Bottles to be found in hole/s:　　　　　　　　　　　　　Number of bottles bought:

Price　　　　　　　　　　Date　　　　　　　　　　Vintage

Grape　　　　　　　　　　Region　　　　　　　　　　Country

Producer

Purchased from

Critical comment

Date opened　　　　　　　　　　　　　　　　*Affix label*

Served with

Guests

Comments

Mark

25

Wine

Bottles to be found in hole/s: Number of bottles bought:

Price   Date   Vintage

Grape   Region   Country

Producer

Purchased from

Critical comment

Affix label

Date opened

Served with

Guests

Comments

Mark

Wine

Bottles to be found in hole/s: Number of bottles bought:

Price Date Vintage

Grape Region Country

Producer

Purchased from

Critical comment

Date opened

Served with

Affix label

Guests

Comments

Mark

Wine

Bottles to be found in hole/s: .... Number of bottles bought: ....

Price .... Date .... Vintage ....

Grape .... Region .... Country ....

Producer ....

Purchased from ....

Critical comment ....

....

Affix label

Date opened

Served with

Guests

Comments

Mark

Wine

Bottles to be found in hole/s: Number of bottles bought:

Price   Date   Vintage

Grape   Region   Country

Producer

Purchased from

Critical comment

Date opened

Served with

Guests

Comments

Mark

Affix label

Wine

Bottles to be found in hole/s: Number of bottles bought:

Price   Date   Vintage

Grape   Region   Country

Producer

Purchased from

Critical comment

Affix label

Date opened

Served with

Guests

Comments

Mark

Wine

Bottles to be found in hole/s: Number of bottles bought:

Price   Date   Vintage

Grape   Region   Country

Producer

Purchased from

Critical comment

Date opened

Served with   *Affix label*

Guests

Comments

Mark

Wine

Bottles to be found in hole/s: Number of bottles bought:

Price   Date   Vintage

Grape   Region   Country

Producer

Purchased from

Critical comment

Affix label

Date opened

Served with

Guests

Comments

Mark

Wine

Bottles to be found in hole/s: Number of bottles bought:

Price   Date   Vintage

Grape   Region   Country

Producer

Purchased from

Critical comment

Date opened

Served with   Affix label

Guests

Comments

Mark

Wine

Bottles to be found in hole/s: **Number of bottles bought:**

Price   **Date**   **Vintage**

Grape   **Region**   **Country**

Producer

Purchased from

Critical comment

Affix label

Date opened

Served with

Guests

Comments

Mark

Wine

Bottles to be found in hole/s: Number of bottles bought:

Price   Date   Vintage

Grape   Region   Country

Producer

Purchased from

Critical comment

Date opened   *Affix label*

Served with

Guests

Comments

Mark

Wine

Bottles to be found in hole/s: Number of bottles bought:

Price   Date   Vintage

Grape   Region   Country

Producer

Purchased from

Critical comment

Affix label

Date opened

Served with

Guests

Comments

Mark

Wine

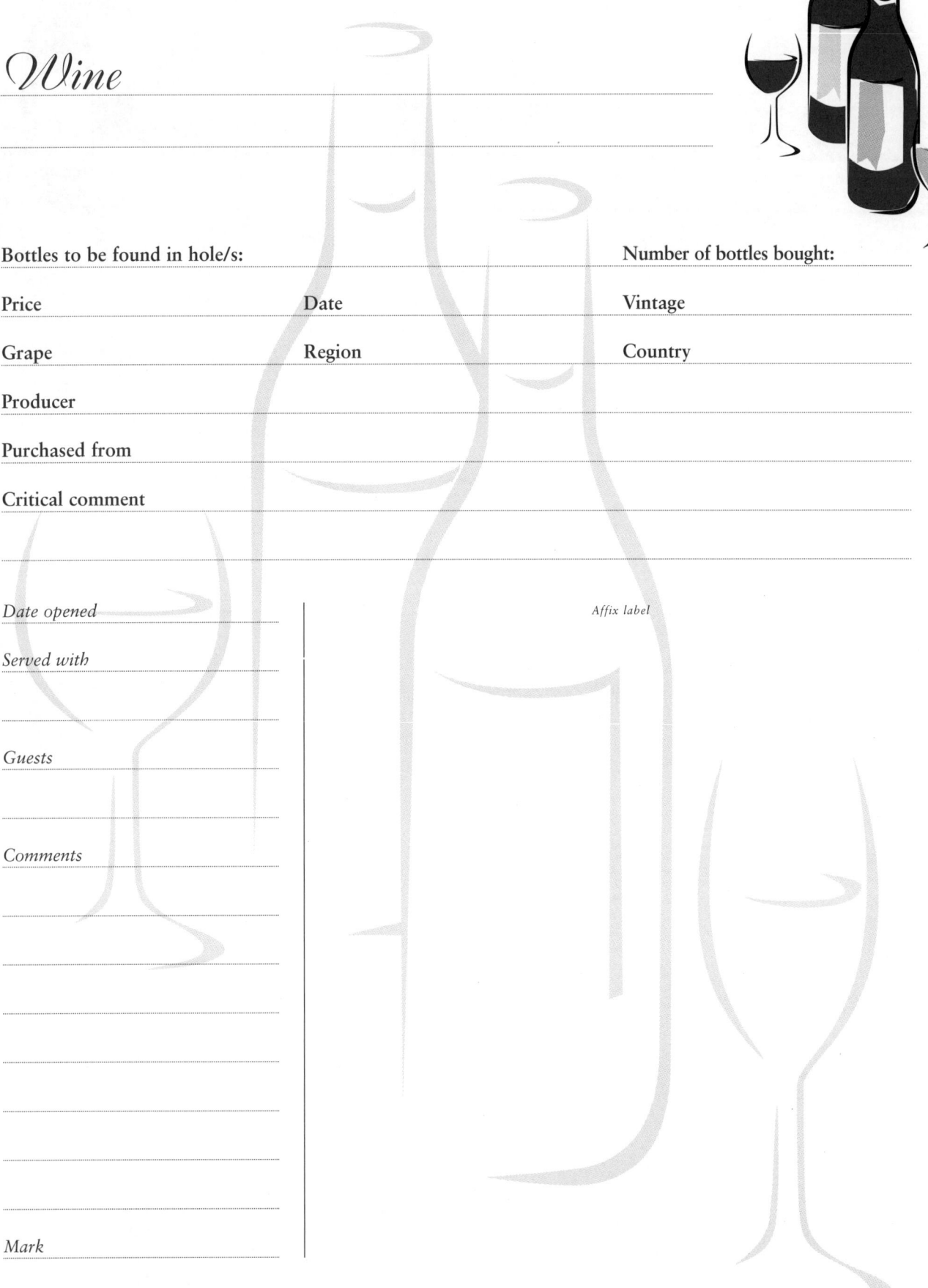

Bottles to be found in hole/s: Number of bottles bought:

Price   Date   Vintage

Grape   Region   Country

Producer

Purchased from

Critical comment

Date opened   *Affix label*

Served with

Guests

Comments

Mark

Wine

Bottles to be found in hole/s:

Number of bottles bought:

Price

Date

Vintage

Grape

Region

Country

Producer

Purchased from

Critical comment

Affix label

Date opened

Served with

Guests

Comments

Mark

Wine

Bottles to be found in hole/s: | Number of bottles bought:

Price | Date | Vintage

Grape | Region | Country

Producer

Purchased from

Critical comment

Date opened

Served with

Affix label

Guests

Comments

Mark

Wine

Bottles to be found in hole/s:　　　　　　　　　　Number of bottles bought:

Price　　　　　　　　　Date　　　　　　　　　　Vintage

Grape　　　　　　　　　Region　　　　　　　　　Country

Producer

Purchased from

Critical comment

Affix label

Date opened

Served with

Guests

Comments

Mark

Wine

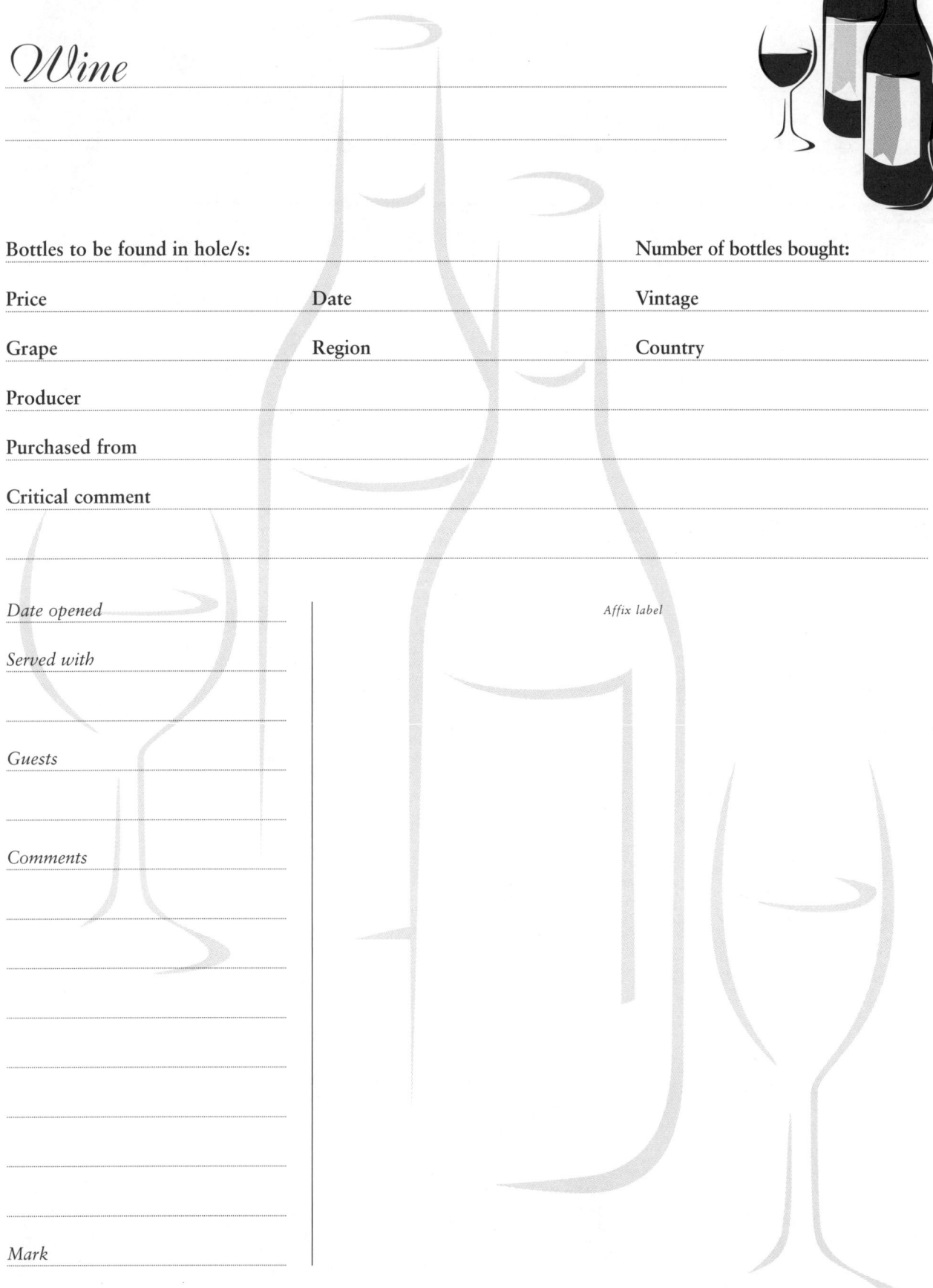

Bottles to be found in hole/s: Number of bottles bought:

Price   Date   Vintage

Grape   Region   Country

Producer

Purchased from

Critical comment

Affix label

Date opened

Served with

Guests

Comments

Mark

Wine

Bottles to be found in hole/s: Number of bottles bought:

Price   Date   Vintage

Grape   Region   Country

Producer

Purchased from

Critical comment

Affix label

Date opened

Served with

Guests

Comments

Mark

Wine

Bottles to be found in hole/s: Number of bottles bought:

Price   Date   Vintage

Grape   Region   Country

Producer

Purchased from

Critical comment

Date opened   *Affix label*

Served with

Guests

Comments

Mark

Wine

Bottles to be found in hole/s: Number of bottles bought:

Price   Date   Vintage

Grape   Region   Country

Producer

Purchased from

Critical comment

Affix label

Date opened

Served with

Guests

Comments

Mark

Wine

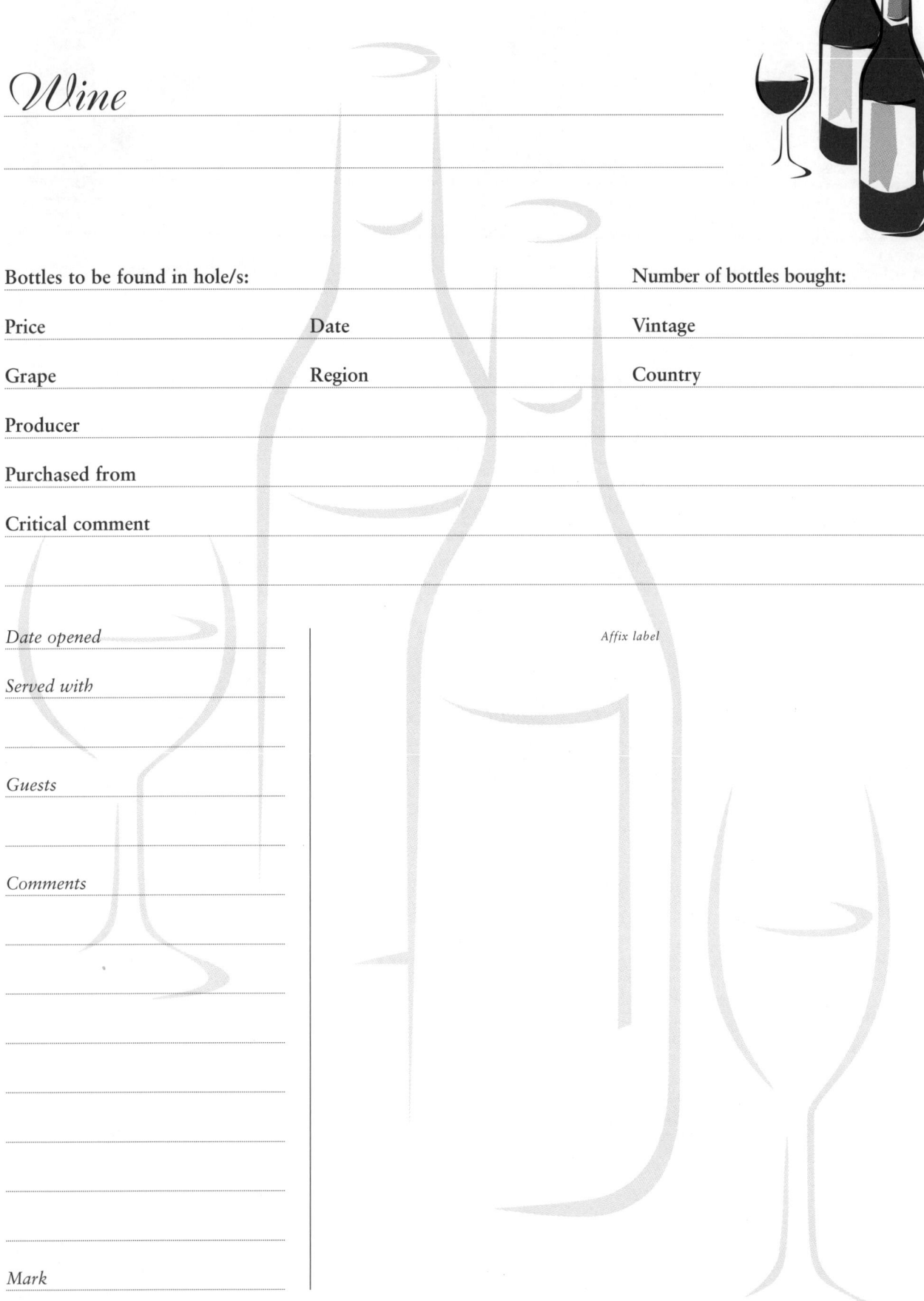

Bottles to be found in hole/s: .... Number of bottles bought: ....

Price .... Date .... Vintage ....

Grape .... Region .... Country ....

Producer ....

Purchased from ....

Critical comment ....
....

Date opened ....

Served with ....
....

Guests ....
....

Comments ....
....
....
....
....
....

Mark ....

Affix label

Wine

Bottles to be found in hole/s:　　　　　　　　　　　　　Number of bottles bought:

Price　　　　　　　　　Date　　　　　　　　　Vintage

Grape　　　　　　　　　Region　　　　　　　　Country

Producer

Purchased from

Critical comment

Affix label

Date opened

Served with

Guests

Comments

Mark

Wine

Bottles to be found in hole/s: Number of bottles bought:

Price   Date   Vintage

Grape   Region   Country

Producer

Purchased from

Critical comment

Date opened

Served with

Guests

Comments

Affix label

Mark

Wine

Bottles to be found in hole/s: ....

Number of bottles bought: ....

Price .... Date ....

Vintage ....

Grape .... Region ....

Country ....

Producer ....

Purchased from ....

Critical comment ....

....

Affix label

Date opened ....

Served with ....

Guests ....

Comments ....

Mark ....

Wine

Bottles to be found in hole/s: Number of bottles bought:

Price   Date   Vintage

Grape   Region   Country

Producer

Purchased from

Critical comment

Date opened   *Affix label*

Served with

Guests

Comments

Mark

Wine

Bottles to be found in hole/s:

Number of bottles bought:

Price　　　　　　　　Date

Vintage

Grape　　　　　　　　Region

Country

Producer

Purchased from

Critical comment

Affix label

Date opened

Served with

Guests

Comments

Mark

Wine

Bottles to be found in hole/s: | Number of bottles bought:

Price | Date | Vintage

Grape | Region | Country

Producer

Purchased from

Critical comment

Date opened | *Affix label*

Served with

Guests

Comments

Mark

Wine

Bottles to be found in hole/s: Number of bottles bought:

Price   Date   Vintage

Grape   Region   Country

Producer

Purchased from

Critical comment

Affix label

Date opened

Served with

Guests

Comments

Mark

Wine

Bottles to be found in hole/s: Number of bottles bought:

Price Date Vintage

Grape Region Country

Producer

Purchased from

Critical comment

Affix label

Date opened

Served with

Guests

Comments

Mark

Wine

Bottles to be found in hole/s:

Number of bottles bought:

Price   Date   Vintage

Grape   Region   Country

Producer

Purchased from

Critical comment

Affix label

Date opened

Served with

Guests

Comments

Mark

Wine

Bottles to be found in hole/s: Number of bottles bought:

Price Date Vintage

Grape Region Country

Producer

Purchased from

Critical comment

Date opened

Served with

Affix label

Guests

Comments

Mark

Wine

Bottles to be found in hole/s: Number of bottles bought:

Price   Date   Vintage

Grape   Region   Country

Producer

Purchased from

Critical comment

Affix label

Date opened

Served with

Guests

Comments

Mark

Wine

Bottles to be found in hole/s: Number of bottles bought:

Price   Date   Vintage

Grape   Region   Country

Producer

Purchased from

Critical comment

Date opened   *Affix label*

Served with

Guests

Comments

Mark

Wine

Bottles to be found in hole/s: Number of bottles bought:

Price   Date   Vintage

Grape   Region   Country

Producer

Purchased from

Critical comment

Affix label

Date opened

Served with

Guests

Comments

Mark

Wine

Bottles to be found in hole/s: Number of bottles bought:

Price   Date   Vintage

Grape   Region   Country

Producer

Purchased from

Critical comment

Date opened   *Affix label*

Served with

Guests

Comments

Mark

Wine

Bottles to be found in hole/s: Number of bottles bought:

Price   Date   Vintage

Grape   Region   Country

Producer

Purchased from

Critical comment

Affix label

Date opened

Served with

Guests

Comments

Mark

Wine

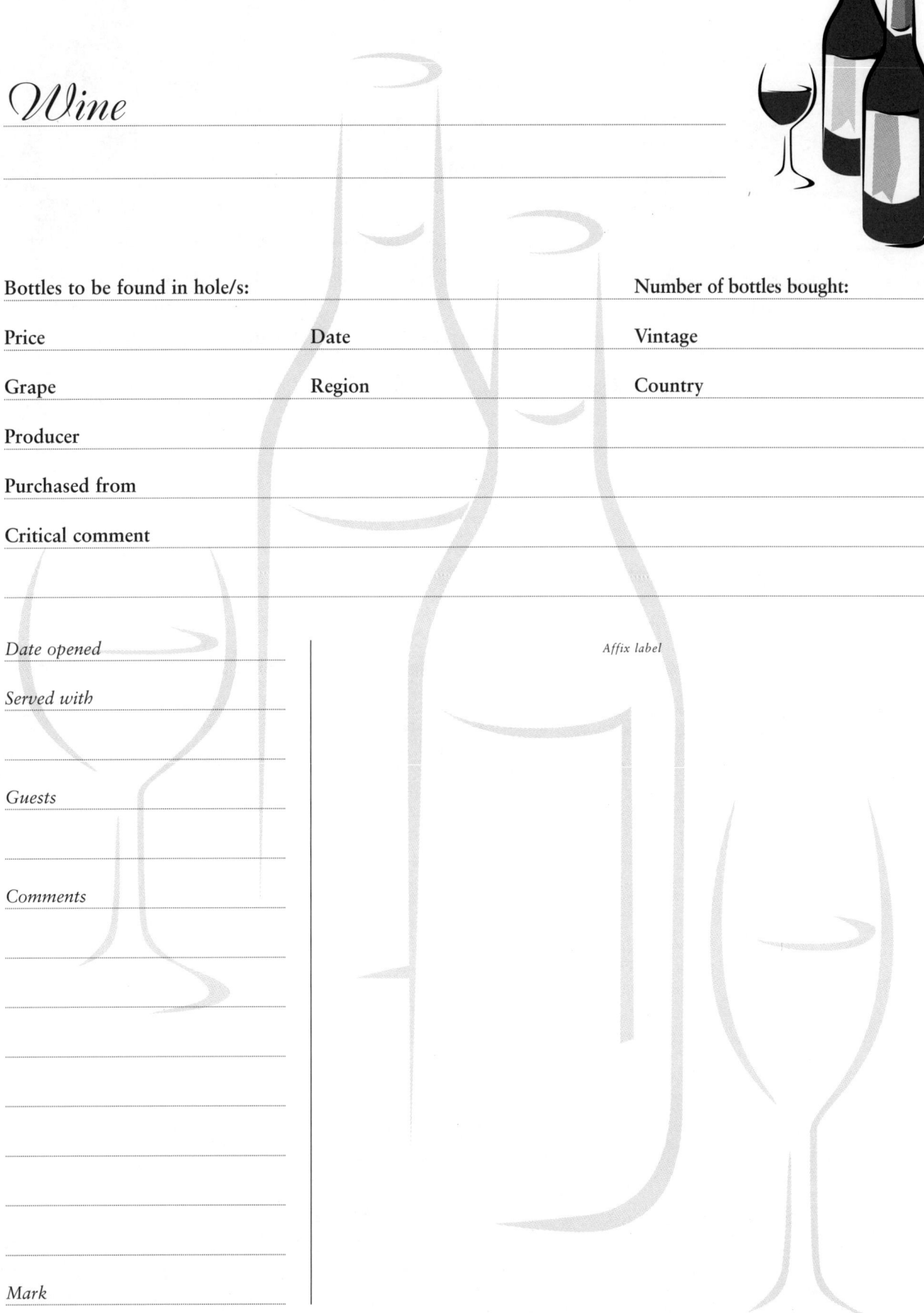

Bottles to be found in hole/s: Number of bottles bought:

Price   Date   Vintage

Grape   Region   Country

Producer

Purchased from

Critical comment

Affix label

Date opened

Served with

Guests

Comments

Mark

Wine

Bottles to be found in hole/s:

Number of bottles bought:

Price   Date   Vintage

Grape   Region   Country

Producer

Purchased from

Critical comment

Affix label

Date opened

Served with

Guests

Comments

Mark

Wine

Bottles to be found in hole/s: Number of bottles bought:

Price   Date   Vintage

Grape   Region   Country

Producer

Purchased from

Critical comment

Date opened

Served with   *Affix label*

Guests

Comments

Mark

Wine

Bottles to be found in hole/s:

Number of bottles bought:

Price Date Vintage

Grape Region Country

Producer

Purchased from

Critical comment

Affix label

Date opened

Served with

Guests

Comments

Mark